THE GRE

ANI

COUR!

BY

ADAIR DIGHTON, F.R.C.S., F.Z.S.

"King Cob" of *The Sportsman*
"Broad Arrow" of *The Sporting Chronicle*

THE EARL AND COUNTESS OF SEFTON WITH SHORTCOMING, THE
WINNER OF THE WATERLOO CUP, 1921.

Preface

THE excuse, if any is necessary, for the publication of another work on "The Greyhound" is that there is no up-to-date book, written on the lines of "Stonehenge's" classic, that contains between its two covers all the information necessary to enable a novice to form a kennel, train his dogs and course them himself.

There is no sport, except perhaps pigeon-racing, that is run on such dead-straight lines as Coursing, and it is this fact that should attract the novice owner to it. Granted a little luck—necessary in everything—he has as much chance, if his dog is good enough, of winning the Waterloo Cup as any other. Some may criticise this and say, or write, that no owner can do this without trainers, walkers, etc. This is wrong, as no sport is so open to the one-dog man as coursing, there is no better exercise, or amusement, than training a greyhound, and I have yet to experience anything more pleasurable or exciting than winning a stake with a home-trained dog. I have been through the game from start to finish and firmly believe that more than half the pleasure lies in doing everything

Preface

—from cleaning out to assisting at whelping—oneself.

I have endeavoured throughout to remember all my own early difficulties and to make them easily understood for others. My medical knowledge and also my connection with *The Sportsman* have naturally been of great assistance.

In conclusion I have to thank Sir Edward Hulton for his kindness in putting the resources of the photographic department of *The Sporting Chronicle* at my disposal, thus enabling me to reproduce a photograph of the final of the 1920 Waterloo, which will live in the memory of all who saw it ; then I have to thank my friend " The Tout " for his kindness and promptitude in turning out a caricature that rivals his very best in aptitude ; then Mr W. H. Twamley for sparing the time to do me a chapter upon " Coursing in Ireland " ; then Mr John Looker for sending me a photograph of King Cob ; and lastly, but by no means the least, I have to thank my friend Mr George Badger for all his trouble and care in typing the MSS. from, I believe, almost indecipherable scribbles. We have been associated before and I hope shall be again.

ADAIR DIGHTON.

WHITCHURCH,
ROSS-ON-WYE.

Contents

List of Illustrations

I

The Early History of Coursing

THE dog of which earliest mention can be found is the greyhound. Solomon, in his Proverbs (chapter xxx., verses 29-31), says :

There be three things which go well, yea, four are comely in going :

A lion which is strongest among beasts, and turneth not away for any ;

A greyhound ; an he goat also ; and a king, against whom there is no rising up.

Thus even in Solomon's time the "long tail" had made its name as a "goer" and was also good to look upon ; and from the picture of Arrian's greyhound Hormé, made over eighteen hundred years ago, and the Lælaps of Ovid, it can be established that the greyhound of those days differed but little from ours of the present day.

All along, the greatest possible care was taken to keep the breed pure. The ancient Greeks took the precaution of having sharp spikes worked into the body clothing of certain breeds to prevent promiscuous connection.

The Greyhound & Coursing

The earliest exhaustive treatise on the greyhound was written by Flavius Arrianus just over eighteen centuries ago. This author assumed the pen-name of Xenophon, and the MSS. of his work lay long in the Vatican under the belief that it was merely an edited Cynegeticus of the older, and better known, Xenophon. The translation of this work was published in 1831 by a gentleman whose *nom de plume*, "A Graduate of Medicine," has, for always, left the coursing world in ignorance of one of its greatest benefactors.

Some of Arrian's dicta are so applicable to modern coursing that one or two may be quoted without excuse. For instance :

"The true Sportsman does not take out his dogs to destroy the Hares, but for the sake of the course, and the contest between the dogs and the Hares, and is glad if the hare escapes."

And again :

". . . they beat the ground in regular array with an extended front proceeding in a straight line to the completion of a certain extent of country, and then wheeling about in a body return in the same way by the side of their former track, omitting as far as possible none of the likely lying."

Then as to the length of slip :

"Whoever has good greyhounds should never lay them in too near the Hare, nor run more than two at a time. For though the animal is very swift and will oftentimes beat the dogs, yet, when she is first started, she is so terrified by the hollo-ing, and by the dogs being very close, that her heart is overcome by fear, and, in the confusion, very often, the best sporting Hares are killed without showing any diversion. She should therefore be suffered to run some distance from her form, and recollect her spirits, and then, if she is a good sporting Hare, she will lift up her ears, and stretch out with long rates from her seat, the dogs directing their course after her with great activity of limb, as if they were leaping, affording a spectacle worthy the trouble that must necessarily be employed in properly breeding and training these dogs."

In reading this last, one can almost imagine the great Arrian with a home-bred-and-trained puppy behind a Southport "stag." Times have altered, but coursing seems to be the same as ever. Still we breed for "speed, endurance, courage and dash"; still we have long slips; still the beaters, and still—as Arrian suggested —a field steward. One is led to wonder whether the Waterloo *really* originated only so late as 1836, or if it was not merely a continuation of an earlier (B.C.) race for which the coveted prize was a laurel wreath instead of a Cup.

The greyhound was introduced to Great Britain probably by the Celts, at the time of their first emigration into Scotland and Ireland, as paintings are known of a Saxon chief and his hunting retinue accompanied by a brace of greyhounds. King John, we are told, took greyhounds in lieu of fines, and Richard II. possessed a greyhound which left him in the hour of his misfortune and attached itself to Bolingbroke—an instance happily rare of a dog's infidelity to its master. It is recorded that the wife of Robert Bruce, when a prisoner of Edward I., had "three men and three women servants, three greyhounds," etc., and Edward, Duke of York, cousin of Richard II., writes of greyhounds in his book, *The Master of Game.*

Dr John Kaye, physician to Edward VI., Mary and Elizabeth, describes these dogs in a book he wrote in Latin on English dogs, and the famous Shane O'Neil presented Lord Robert Duddeley with "two horses, two hawks and two greyhounds" when soliciting him to interest Queen Elizabeth on his behalf. James I. apparently had a large kennel of them, and in the *Book of Sports*, published at the end of his reign, rules with regard to Slipping are given.

In the reign of Queen Elizabeth an attempt to put the sport on a proper footing was made, and rules were drawn up by the Duke of Norfolk which remained in force more or less until the close of the last century. For much of the sporting history of that time we are indebted to Gervase Markham, who, in his book, *Country Contentments*, provides a fund of information of present interest. He writes :

" Now after your dog comes to full growth, as at a year and a half, or two years old, he would then have a fine long lean head, with a sharp nose, rush grown from the eye downwards : a full clear eye with long eyelids, a sharp ear, short and close falling, a long neck a little binding, with a loose handing wezand, a broad breast, straight forelegs, side hollow, ribs straight, a square and flat back, short and strong fillets, a broad space between the hips, a strong stearn or tayl and a round foot and good large clefts."

He is the first writer on the feeding of greyhounds of whom we have any record, and, forgetting that there has been a war, his diets approximate to modern standards and with little change might be found in most kennels. He writes :

" The best general Food for the upholding of a Dog in a good state is, chippings, crusts of bread, soft tender bones or gristle of Veal, Lamb, or such like, first scalded in Beef broth not very salt, or other broths in which have been boyled Mutton, Veal or Venison or any kind of Pollen ; or for want thereof other clean scalding water, after your chippings or bread is scalded you shall let it stand and cool, then when your feeding hour cometh, you shall take as much good milk, flotten milk or buttermilk (but the best is most wholesome) as will fully or more whiten the same : for it is to be intended that your water must be all drunk up into your bread, and your milk must only make it swim."

His directions for exercise were somewhat heroic, but these were followed even into the nineteenth century, as " Stonehenge," in his book on *The Greyhound*, commends gallops of four miles at top speed, whereas nowadays six furlongs, at the most, is considered a useful gallop.

The first meeting of which an account is given took place at Swaffham, in Norfolk, in 1776, and was promoted by the celebrated Lord Orford. This was followed by Ashdown Park in 1780 and Malton Coursing Club in 1781. These early clubs were probably responsible for the present-day fashion, in coursing nomenclature, of naming dogs after their owners' initials, as the membership of these clubs was often limited to twenty-six, each member being allocated a letter which had to be the first letter in the name of his dog.

Lord Orford, the founder of the Swaffham Club, was probably the first breeder to try the bull-dog cross to which the brindle colour is supposed to trace. His favourite greyhound was Czarina, who won forty-seven matches and was never beaten, and who, at the age of thirteen years, gave birth to Claret, sire of the immortal Snowball. A melancholy interest is attached to Czarina, as Lord Orford, mounted as usual on his piebald pony, fell dead after she had won her last course.

Ashdown Park coursing meetings were originated by Lord Craven, whose gamekeeper, Parker, used to slip the dogs from horseback and carried a small white stick with which to control the too great energy of the dogs. He slipped his dogs at a gallop, so, in addition to being a good slipper, he must have been pretty useful on a horse ! Another Ashdown novelty was the putting of a hare in a trap, and after allowing a certain amount of liberty the greyhounds were slipped and the first up won. Goodlake, writing of this, says :

"The above system, which we have never seen or heard of being put into practice at any other club, appears to us to be admirably adapted to show the strength and speed of the greyhound ;

it was found, too, to give an interest to many who did not feel any excitement in the wilder sport."

This novelty was soon discontinued, as it was of no value except as a criterion of pace, and, like the later enclosed coursing, did nothing to improve—in fact, rather the opposite—the breed.

No one particular person can be associated with the formation of the Malton Club, though the list of members included the names of the Duke of Gordon, Lord Macdonald, etc., and Major Popham's Snowball won the Cup twice.

About this time a distinguished member of the Coursing world was Miss Ann Richards, of Compton Beauchamp. She, we are told, was beautiful, was blessed with plenty of "the needful" and inherited a large landed estate, but nothing could tempt her to anything that might in the very least interfere with her love of cours- ing, and many scores of disappointed suitors were turned away. She wrote her own epitaph, which was found amongst her papers at her death.

Louth Coursing Society was formed in 1806, and had as secretary Mr Adam Eve, who, as a wag remarked, was descended on both sides from the oldest families in England. Ilsley came into being in the same year and Derbyshire Coursing Society some nine years later : Newmarket came in about the same time, but, as at present, its existence was fitful, though its Gold Cup was the first at stake in this country.

After Lord Orford's time the bull-dog cross was tried again by Lord Rivers, and the produce of this cross were undoubtedly the ancestors of King Cob. There are many opinions for and against this cross, and it must not be forgotten that Blue Hat, Patent and Chloe were all descended from it. The first-named gets it through Czar, who was descended from Eurus in tail female, the second-named from Egypt, and the third from Lopez. It was tried again later, but was not successful.

Beacon Hill was formed in 1812, Morfe in 1815 and Deptford in 1819. Amesbury followed in 1822 and was a meeting that deserves special mention. It was run on the Downs, near Stonehenge, and the hares were noted for their stoutness. The Druid Cup was the chief event, and it was here that in 1864 the Altcar Club challenged the World to produce sixteen bitch puppies, sixteen dog puppies and sixteen all-aged greyhounds to beat sixteen of each which they would produce. The Club won the Challenge Bracelet for bitch puppies, with two left in ; the World won the Challenge Bracelet for dog puppies, with two left in ; and the Club scored a big win in the All-Aged Challenge Cup by having all the last four that were left in. The meeting extended over seven days, and

The Greyhound & Coursing

Mr Warwick, the judge, estimated that he rode at least a hundred and thirty miles on the last day. He changed horses four times and every one of them had had enough. It is worthy of note that Bit of Fashion was beaten in the decider of the All-Aged race by Cheer Boys.

Passing over the Deptford Union Club, established in 1826, and Burton-on-Trent in 1825, one comes to the still pre-eminent Altcar Club —and what history its annals contain ! It was founded in 1825 by Lord Molyneux, as great a name in Coursing as that of Derby on the Turf, and the members dined at the Waterloo Hotel in Liverpool, the site of which is now occupied by the Central Station. The Altcar Cup for puppies was first run for at the February meeting of 1828, and was won by, appropriately, Lord Molyneux's Milo. The names of the members are in many cases the same as they are to-day : such as Hornby, Blundell, Hesketh and Heywood need no bibliography in to-day's *Coursing Who's Who.*

The Ridgeway was a later club, coming into existence about 1830. According to the exhaustive searches of David Brown, this club was probably formed as a continuation of, or an amalgamation with, Southport. At one of the first meetings, held near Newton-le-Willows, to which " all the clergy of the district and all the leading County families were invited," a professional judge in Mr David Brown, of Falkirk, officiated, and for the first time wore scarlet, and followed the dogs in true hunting fashion. (This was not the David Brown who goes down to fame as the Editor of the *Greyhound Stud Book*.) The Ridgeway Club instituted a field costume for its members in 1831–1832, which consisted of a green cloth frock-coat, drab vest, corduroy breeches, and long leather boots coming well up the legs. The meetings were held at Southport over the Scarisbrick estates, at Lytham over the famous Clifton estates, and at Fleetwood over Sir Hesketh Fleetwood's estates. Mr Ridgeway, the originator, was first President, to be followed by his son, Mr T. Ridgeway, and then by Mr Hardman and Mr Heywood Jones, of Liverpool. Next, in 1872, was Mr Clifton of Clifton, Blackpool, who was succeeded by Mr Mallabey. Mr Ridgeway won the Cup in December 1830 with John Allan, and his son won it two years in succession, 1840–1841, with Princess Royal, who in the first year beat a litter brother, Exciseman, in the final.

Now for the Scottish clubs. The earliest was the Midlothian, which was founded in 1811, and consisted of twenty ordinary members and ten honorary members. It was said that no one lower than a baronet could be elected as a member, and every member brought his own dish to the dinner. Thus, according to *The*

Druid, "the Duke of Buccleuch sent venison, Sir Graham Montgomery a haunch of black-face wether; Major Hamilton Douglas black puddings and haggis; Mr W. Sharpe ducks of eight or nine pounds in weight; Lord Melville pork; Mr Callender beef; Mr Wauchope, perigord pie, and so on." Mr Nightingale judged twenty-nine consecutive meetings, and preferred it to the Waterloo Meeting, remarking: "It made no matter if the coursing was a little dull at times, there was always the view." We are not told whether he referred to the landscape or the dinner! The name of this club was changed to the Roman Camp Club.

One of the most progressive of the early meetings was that of the Lanarkshire and Renfrewshire Club, whose patron was Sir John Maxwell. It was here that coloured flags were first introduced, and also printed field-cards. The judge had to follow immediately behind the dogs and keep with them all the time, and then deliver his verdict in an audible voice to the flag steward. The present-day slips originated at this meeting, being made, and invented, by a Paisley gunsmith. A pair came into the possession of Sir Hesketh Fleetwood, who took them to Altcar, Ashdown and Newmarket, and this was the original model of the slips in current use, which have been altered but not improved. Another original custom in vogue

here was that at the large Annual Meeting there
was an interval of one day's rest "to put those
dogs having severe courses on a par with those
having short, and afford them a fair chance in the
deciding course, and test their true merits."
Puppy stakes were confined to those not above
twenty months old, all over that age being
classed with old dogs.

Another early Scottish meeting was that of
Ardrossan, which came into existence at least as
early as 1818, as David Brown in his famous
article, *Historical Sketch of Coursing*, relates how
he came across a pair of silver dog couples
inscribed as follows :—" The Ardrossan Coursing
Prize, won by William Blair, Esq., of Blair's
blue dog Spring 5th March 1818." Ardrossan
was at its zenith when Lord Eglinton successfully challenged England with his dog Waterloo,
first beating a Cumberland dog in a match for
£200 at Annbank and then Mr Goodlake's
Gracchus in a match for two hundred guineas—
the best of three courses from Compton Bottom
in the Ashdown country. Ardrossan fell into
abeyance from 1848 to 1854, and was finally
wound up in 1880 because of the shortage of
hares. This has been the cause of many of
the older meetings dropping out, and was responsible for the "winding up" of Biggar, Roman
Camp, Upper Annandale, etc.

The Biggar Club sprang into being some time

The Greyhound & Coursing

just previous to 1800 and became the Biggar, or Upper Ward of Lanarkshire Coursing Club in 1825. The Club ran well until 1847, when, owing to some unpleasantness, Mr Paterson, the secretary, withdrew, and though a committee tried to manage its affairs, it eventually amalgamated with the Caledonian Club under the name of the Scotch National Coursing Club.

One of the very first of the Scottish clubs was Dirleton and North Berwick, which must be mentioned, as its rules contained one which read : " No trial shall be considered a course if it is found that the hare coursed is a three-legged one " ; and in one of the big stakes an appeal was made to the National Club, who declined to recognise the rule and gave the stake in conformity with the judge's decision.

This brings coursing down to the time of the establishment of the National Coursing Club in 1858, which has become as authoritative a body in the Coursing world as the Jockey Club has on the Turf. The National Club formed a committee of three, consisting of Mr Edward Marjoribanks, the President ; Mr Borron (the owner of Beacon, who, mated with Scotland Yet, hands down his fame with Canaradzo, Coorooran, Sea Foam, Sea Pink and King Death ; and when mated with Polly, got Roaring Meg, the '62 Waterloo winner) ; and Mr J. H. Walsh, who goes down to history as

24

"A DREAM OF THE WATERLOO CUP." AFTER THE BANQUET
Specially drawn by "The Tout"

JOE BARNET   LORD SEFTON   MR. M. L. HEARN   MR. S. BEER   MR. DYKE DENNIS
MR. H. BROCKLEBANK   MR. LAMONBY   MR. O. ASCHE
MR. HOPKINS   MR. MUGLISTON   LORD LONSDALE   MR. WALKER
                                                THE DUKE OF LEEDS MR. HUGH PEEL
        LORD ENNISKILLEN   SIR R. B. JARDINE
                            MR. HARRISON

the foremost coursing writer of all time. His *nom de plume* of "Stonehenge" for years hid his real self, but his work was of such a high standard that no pseudonym could stand it, and his book, *Stonehenge on the Greyhound*, is still the courser's classic. These three gentlemen had the drawing up of the rules allotted to them, and in those days this was indeed a difficult task, as there were many ways by which the knowing ones tried to ensure the judge's verdict being satisfactory to themselves. As one owner of that time said : " I had a good kennel of greyhounds once, and I could do no more than make expenses. And," he added, with satisfaction, " I was clever, too, as I had nothing but black ones and managed to change them when one was hard run."

In 1882 the *Stud Book* appeared, and soon afterwards a regulation was passed that no dog could be registered without a pedigree, and no dog could be entered at any meeting unless he was registered in the *Stud Book*. This ensured correct pedigrees and a knowledge of the dog that was running, and overcame such abuses as substitution, renaming, etc., which were all too common in the early days.

As "Enclosed Coursing" has long ceased to exist in England, it may be as well to treat of it here, though it still has a great vogue in Ireland.

In the year 1877 a farmer at Plumpton, near

Brighton—a Mr Case—started the first enclosed meeting as a commercial venture. He enclosed a stretch of land with wire-netting at considerable expense, for breeding purposes, and laid down two fields as running tracks, with an artificial cover at the end of each, into which the hares were driven before coursing commenced. At the other end of the field an ingenious escape fence was erected, which enabled the hare to elude her pursuers and to end the course. Each running field was about six hundred yards in length.

The provisions of the Hares and Rabbits Bill, which passed in 1880, had a great deal to do with the temporary popularity of enclosed coursing. This Bill gave a tenant an equal right with his landowner to ground game on his holding. This gave the farmer a right to shoot, trap, or snare hares, of which so many took advantage that many small country meetings had to "stop down" on account of shortage of hares.

The principal event at Plumpton was the Street Place Stakes, which was won in the first year by Master Banrigh. The first fixture was such a success that in the following year the Southern Cup for thirty-two all-ages at £10, 10s. each was instituted and eight ex-Waterloo dogs went to the slips. These were Dark Rustic, Kilkenny, Serapis, Huron, Sir

Magnus, Conster, The Squatter and Hugh
Gillespie, the stake resulting in a division
between Dark Rustic and Early Morn. The
next year a further enlargement was made,
as the Cup became the Great Southern Cup
at £12, 10s. each, and attracted sixty-four
entries, the winner taking £250 and a piece
of plate value £50. Mr Darlinson's Deceit
won, and Woodland King ran up. Though
Lord Lurgan, Captain Archdale, Duke of
Hamilton, Lord St Vincent and Sir John
Astley supported these meetings, many, or
most, of the true coursers would have nothing
to do with it, and in 1889 it came to an end.
Gosforth, designed by Mr Case, followed
Plumpton and was well supported. The
chief prize here was the Gosforth Gold Cup,
which reached the same value as the Plumpton Cup and attracted many of the best dogs
in the country. In 1885 Mineral Water—
the 1884 Waterloo winner—won, and in 1886
Cangaroo, one of the fastest dogs ever slipped,
beat Greentick, the '84 runner-up. Then in
1887 Mullingar beat Huic Halloa, who had
won the Gosforth Derby, and in 1888 the
latter dog went one better in winning from
Burnaby, who had just previously taken the
Waterloo. In 1889 Gosforth was abandoned.

Kempton Park commenced in 1883, but
only lasted until 1889, and was then also

abandoned. The chief winner of its "star turn," The Champion Stakes, was Huic Halloa, who won from Greater Scot in 1887.

Haydock Park was more successful, and will always be remembered as the meeting at which Fullerton made his debut. Herschel also made his name there by taking the Produce Stakes and, in that season (1887), he went on to win the Sefton Stakes at Altcar, divide the Waterloo Cup with Greater Scot, and then divide the Members Plate at Altcar — a great performance for a puppy! In the following year he won the Champion Stakes from Huic Halloa after leading him, a fast dog, nearly four lengths to his hare. The last meeting at Haydock was held in 1889 and was a fiasco, as, although the entries were only thirty-six in number, the full stake money had to be found, and the directors were very badly hit.

Other enclosed meetings were Wye, Four Oaks, Birmingham and Doncaster, which only survived two meetings. Enclosed coursing only had a brief life in England, but in that time it undoubtedly did a great deal of harm, as dogs were bred for pace, and pace alone, without any thought of working powers. Hares, at the enclosed meetings, knew the way into the field, and also, even better, knew the way out. From start to finish it was merely a race, and the fast, flashy dog was always too good for the really genuine worker. Mr Porter, quoted in the Badminton volume on *Coursing*, wrote :

" Now that enclosed coursing is losing popularity all must see the ruin that has arisen from it : good greyhounds spoiled ; fluky flashy ones benefited ; stamina and determination lost sight of ; etc."

Ireland still has enclosed meetings, notably at Massarene Park and Cork, but the result is seen when their dogs come over here for the big races like the Waterloo. They may be faster than ours—in fact, usually are— but when it comes to working they go wide, get their heads in the air, and are useless. Take that " flier" of recent years, Lord Protector : he was without question one of the fastest dogs in Harmonicon's Cup, but was " all wings " when it came to work and was lucky to even win a course.

II

The Waterloo Cup

WHAT the Derby is to racing men the "Waterloo" is to coursing men; hence, with the coming of February in each year, the daily papers are filled with references to the "blue ribbon of the leash," the "plains of Altcar," etc., in much the same way as they are with the "blue ribbon of the Turf" a month or two later.

The Waterloo Cup is one of the red-letter days in Liverpool's year, yet turning up their annals for the year 1836 I can find no reference to the fact that, in that year, a Mr Lynn, the proprietor of the Waterloo Hotel, got up an eight-dog stake which he styled "The Waterloo Cup," and which was run for over Lord Sefton's estate at Altcar. In the following year this race was enlarged to one for sixteen runners, and in 1838 to one for thirty-two, at which number it remained until 1857, when it was made a sixty-four-dog stake, and continues so to the present day.

In the first year the entry fee was £2, and the winner received a silver snuff-box, in addition to the stakes. With the increase of the nominations to sixteen, the entry fee rose to £5, remaining at that until the "thirty-two-dog" era, when it rose to £25, at which figure it remains to-day.

For the entry fee of £25 the nominator gets a chance of winning :

"*The Waterloo Cup* (with cup value £100 added by the Earl of Sefton) for sixty-four subscribers at £25 each ; winner £500, second £200, two dogs £50 each, four dogs £30 each, eight dogs £20 each, sixteen dogs £10 each."

"*The Waterloo Purse* of £215 taken from the Cup Stakes, for the thirty-two dogs beaten in the first round of the Cup ; winner £75, second £30, two dogs £15 each, four dogs £10 each, eight dogs £5 each."

"*The Waterloo Plate* of £145 taken from the Cup Stakes, for the sixteen dogs beaten in the first ties of the Cup ; winner £75, second £30, two dogs £10 each, four dogs £5 each."

From this it can be seen that only sixteen dogs fail to gain a prize, and that if an owner has a dog of any use he can hardly fail to get his money back.

The first year's race was won by Milanie, a red bitch by Milo *ex* Duchess, appropriately enough the property of Lord Molyneux, afterwards Lord Sefton, and nominated by Mr Lynn, the organiser of the race. The runner-up was Unicus, a black dog, the property of Mr Norris, by Hornet out of Fly. In 1837 Fly, a black bitch, by Tommy Roads *ex* Fly, beat Dr Fop, and Bugle won the Derby Stakes from a dog of Mr Lynn's, in Topper.

The Derby Stakes in the following year became the Altcar Stakes, which in 1857 became the Waterloo Purse, and the Waterloo Plate was added. Bugle, a blue, won the Cup in 1838 from Risk, and was one of the earliest winners that appears with frequency in present-day pedigrees. He was the sire of Stave dam of Bluelight sire of Beacon, who will always be remembered for his combination with that marvel Scotland Yet, which produced Canaradzo, Sea Foam, etc. The next year another bitch, Empress, won and beat her own brother Sultan. "She was a very handsome squary bitch, with lots of wear and tear, and good all round." By Tramp out of Nettle, she belonged to Mr Robinson, and took the Cup from another bitch, Brenda.

In 1840 Mr Easterbury owned the winner and runner-up (a feat not repeated until 1859) in Earwig and Emperor, and declared Earwig, the worst of the two, the winner. Both these dogs were black, but one had a white end to his tail, a white nose and claw. Emperor added to his winnings on the field by becoming a really great sire, siring such dogs as Priam, winner in 1842, and Harlequin, in 1846. The following year saw probably the worst dog that ever won the " Waterloo " win in Bloomsbury, with such dogs behind him as Waterloo, the first to connect Lord Eglinton's name with the race, and Saddler.

In 1842 Priam, a fawn-and-white dog by Emperor, won. He was 74 lb. in weight, and yet was a first-rate worker and never gave a chance away. He was perhaps the best big dog of his day, and there have not been many since of his weight that have combined size and working powers. Other heavy dogs that have won have been Selby, who weighed 75 lb. and won in 1859 ; Sackcloth, 73½ lb., the winner in 1854, and Harmonicon, 70 lb., who beat Hopsack for the last Waterloo run prior to the European War. The pace and work necessary to win a Waterloo are not as a rule combined with weight.

The year 1843 saw Major take the Cup from Solon. Sandy, sire of Speculation, the winner in 1844, ran up to Zurich for the Stakes. In 1845 Titania, " a good steady bitch, but not a great one," won from Sherwood. The above quotation from *The Druid* respecting her abilities may have been the opinion of that time, but when one remembers that she was, at the time of winning, a second-season bitch and had left a litter, by Tom Tough, only four months previously, it can hardly be the opinion that would be given to-day. She had run well the previous year, only being beaten in the fourth round by Dressmaker, the runner-up to Speculation.

In 1846 a son of Emperor, Harlequin, won from Oliver Twist, entirely on account of his steadiness. Oliver Twist was a litter brother to Senate, winner in 1847, and was one of that lucky litter owned by Lord Sefton which was bred from Sadek ex Sanctity. These dogs were not up to form and were weeded out for "dumping" when Sanctity came in season and they were bred together, with the result of Oliver Twist, Senate and Eastham. "Oliver was a great dog, and a wonderful killer." He once won a seventy-four dog stake at Lytham, without once being challenged, and killed every hare. In the next year, 1847, his brother Senate won from Flirt, a bitch by Marquis ex Coquette, who was at the time of the race carrying a litter by the famous Foremost. Senate was a bad killer but went a very fair pace and could keep going on, and a week before his Waterloo had run a hare at Lytham for a quarter of an hour. According to *The Druid*, he was "a wandy dog, full of muscle, and his wrenching had always this grand peculiarity, that he did not wrench too hard, did not put them too far round, but gave no opening and kept the game to himself."

CERITO, MOCKING BIRD AND HUGHIE GRAHAM
From a picture in the Author's Collection

LOBELIA, MASTER M'GRATH AND BAB-AT-THE-BOWSTER
From a picture In the Author's Collection

The Waterloo Cup

In 1848 and 1849 two of Sir St Gore's dogs in Shade and Magician won. The former, by Nonchalance, was a black-and-white and beat another of the same colour, Smut, by Sam, the famous Newmarket dog owned by Mr Gibson. Nonchalance was by King Cob, the property of Captain Daintree and the first Newmarket dog to be advertised at public Stud. This dog, King Cob, was the sire of Figaro and The Tollwife, who were, respectively, sire of Bedlamite, Humming Bird, Mocking Bird, etc., and dam of Motley—sire of David, and of Mrs Kitty Brown—dam of Clara dam of Chloe.

The runner-up was Forward, by Foremost, King Cob's greatest rival at the Stud. Czar, afterwards to become famous at Stud, litter brother to Forward, ran up for the Altcar Stakes.

The next winner was that little wonder, Cerito, who ranks with Master M'Grath and Fullerton as thrice winner of the Cup. In her case the Cup was only for thirty-two dogs, but all the same her performance must be classed as one of the most meritorious of all time. She was whelped in 1848, stood 25 inches in height, weighed 51 lb., and was fawn and white.

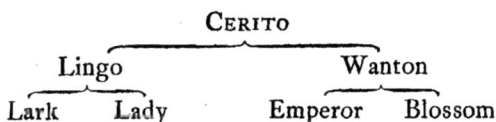

CERITO

	Lingo		Wanton	
Lark	Lady		Emperor	Blossom

35

The Greyhound & Coursing

Her first course was as a puppy, in 1849, when, running under the name of Lucy Long, she was beaten by Banker in the first round of the Cockerham Hall Cup. This was in October, and in the following February she won four courses at Broughton, being beaten in the fifth course by Blueskin, the winner. After this she was sold for a fabulous price and her name changed to Cerito, under which she won her first Waterloo the same month, beating Neville in the final. The next month she was beaten at an Altcar Club meeting by Sefton, and then retired until the following season. In October she was drawn lame after her first course at the Wiltshire Champion meeting, and in December won the Ridgeway Challenge Cup and Stakes. Following on this she was beaten in the fourth round of the Broughton Cup by Voltigeur, the winner, and then went on to Altcar to be beaten in the first round of the Cup by Jamie Forest, but ran up to Dalton, after a terrific course, for the Altcar Stakes. This year, 1851, the Cup went to Hughie Graham, a fawn dog by Liddesdale out of Queen of the May by King Cob. His best course was that for the final with Staymaker. He got badly off from the slips, and Staymaker, one of Foremost's sons, led for the early part of a long run-up, but Hughie Graham got up inch by inch and took the turn with his head in front. He then used his hare for two or three wrenches and then turned her to Staymaker to kill. He had another heavy course with that wonderful bitch, Mocking Bird, who was third. This was a bitch that wanted a very stout hare that she could use all the time, as she had tons of pluck and stayed on for ever, but was not a great worker.

The next year, 1852, Cerito again won the Cup, this time from Larriston, who had beaten Hughie Graham in the second course. Mocking Bird was also beaten in the second round, by Stanley, who went down to Cerito in the third. In 1853 the little bitch recorded her third win, beating Movement in the final. This was her last race, and she retired to the Stud, having won forty-five out of fifty-three courses, and with the nice total of £1000 to her credit, besides three Cups, the Ridgeway Challenge Cup and Crenoline Picture. She had grand pace, and as a killer there was nothing like her for safety and science. Her timing was perfection. She never made a flying kill, but seemed to draw herself back, wait for the turn and then, like a shot from a gun, with one movement hold and kill.

A great little bitch that must always go down to history as one of the best ever slipped.

In 1854 Sackcloth beat Larriston and won

for Lord Sefton, and in 1855 Judge won for Mr Jefferson under the nomination of Mr Brocklebank. This was a really great dog and, in the final, he beat a really great bitch in Scotland Yet, and the two have left their names in greyhound pedigrees in a way that no dog, before or since, has ever accomplished. Judge sired Clive, winner in 1859 ; Maid of the Mill, winner in 1860, and Chloe, winner in 1863. Scotland Yet, mated with Beacon—by Bluelight —produced Canaradzo, who won the Cup in 1861 and was sire of King Death, who took it in 1864; Sea Foam, the sire of Lobelia, who won the Cup in 1867 ; Bugle, the grandsire of Sea Cove, the winner in 1870, and Coorooran. Judge was a great worker once settled, and Scotland Yet one of the sweetest of runners : starting slowly, she stole along with that perfect effortless action that is so telling in a long course, and then shot out to kill in once.

The next year, 1856, the last as a thirty-two dog race, saw Judge beaten in the final, after running an undecided, by Protest, a fawn bitch, the property of Mr D. Peacock.

In 1857 the Cup was increased to sixty-four dogs ; the Altcar Stakes became the Purse and the Waterloo Plate was added. This arrangement continued without a break until the year 1917, when, out of respect to the feeling of the public, all three races were abandoned.

The Waterloo Cup

The first year it was run as a sixty-four-dog race, the Cup was won by a white-and-fawn dog, King Lear, who beat a red-hot favourite in Sunbeam in the final. This latter dog was one of the hottest favourites that ever ran for the Waterloo, but was badly handicapped for the final as he had had a dreadful doing in his course with Tempest on the same day. After running him to a standstill, he got on to a fresh hare, which he coursed on his own to Hill House. The Purse went to Albatross, who beat David in the final. David was sire of Patent, who, though never winning a Waterloo, was a really great dog, cool and steady and a certain killer. One of his cleverest kills was when he actually killed whilst jumping a fence at Tredegar. After being beaten for the Waterloo, he won three Cups in a month at Hereford, Ashdown and the Scottish National. Like David, he never tired. Neville, a rank outsider, won in the following year, and extraordinarily, at least according to present-day ideas, was sire of Dr Dodd, who ran up to Albatross, who took the Purse for the second time. Nowadays one seldom hears of dogs winning races after being used at Stud, or of bitches coursing after having had litters, but in the olden times it seems to have been nothing very much out of the common.

The year 1859 was chiefly remarkable for the

fact that for the first time the race was divided.
The dividers, Clive and Selby, were both the
property of Mr J. Jardine. Clive was a black
bitch by Judge and Selby a black dog by Barrator.
This was the first of Judge's progeny to win,
and Maid of the Mill repeated it the next year.
She was a fine big racing bitch and fairly ran
rings round Blue Hat in an early course, and
won with plenty in hand of Sampler in the
final.

1861 saw the first of the Beacon—Scotland
Yet combination in Canaradzo win. He had
fine pace and working power and was particularly
clever in closing with his hare. In his Waterloo
he gave Faldonside "a regular towelling" and
it was only by favour that Gilbert took the turn
when they met. He has proved greater at Stud
than he did on the field, as, as sire of King Death
and, through Boanerges, grandsire of Bab-at-the-
Bowster, he has left a name often conjured with.
His litter sister Cioloja was, at home, better
than he and went through a thirty-two-dog
stake at Sudbury, only giving one point away
throughout her courses. After this she was a
hot favourite for the Cup, but unluckily broke
her leg in an exercise gallop two or three days
beforehand. There are many slips between the
entry and the Cup in a Waterloo.

Another of Beacon's get in Roaring Meg won
from Bowfell in 1862, and Sea Pink, one of the

Beacon—Scotland Yet litter, won the Purse. Roaring Meg was not a really great bitch, but very determined and a good worker, whilst Sea Pink had a very bad temper and was apt to run very wild at times. Chloe, by Judge ex Clara, took the race in 1863 from Rebe. A well-made bitch, she was a little slow from the slips, but was faster than Rebe in the stretches, worked better and used her teeth well. She ran again in the following year, but was beaten in the second round of the Cup and again in the Plate. Mated with King Death, the winner in 1864, she threw Chameleon, who won the Purse in 1872. Rebe was one of the most genuine but most unlucky bitches that ever ran, as, after running up to Chloe in 1863, she repeated it in 1864 behind King Death, who only just held her. Then in 1865 she divided the Purse, and in 1866 was in the last four of Brigadier's Cups. She was one of the pluckiest bitches that ever ran at Altcar, and could go fast, and also had a trick of being able to take a drain, stop, turn and take it back whilst her opponent was usually "all wings" on the other side. In 1864 the first member of the medical profession to take a Waterloo, Dr Richardson, won with the somewhat sarcastically named King Death, by Canaradzo, who won the Plate the following year, when Meg the outsider won the Cup from King Tom, another of Canaradzo's sons.

The Greyhound & Coursing

One of those rare "turn ups" came off in 1866, as Brigadier won. He had previously shown wretched form, and was purchased for twenty-five shillings. He ran really well all through the Cup and was never challenged, except once by Fieldfare, who jumped over him to get in. He afterwards sired a first-class bitch in Brigade, who, according to *The Druid*, was a better bitch than Jane Anne, who won the Purse in 1868, and Bab-at-the-Bowster, the runner-up to Master M'Grath in 1869. Cheap winners are one of the fascinations of coursing, but, though more often heard about, are not so frequent as expensive losers. We have all had dogs for nothing that have won good races, and at the moment I myself have one for which I gave £2, and paid no railway fare at that, who has already won one race and can go on winning more, but she does not counterbalance the beautifully bred puppies that after two years' feeding cannot find pace enough to keep themselves warm. It's a great game, but there's no "money for nothing" in it. Strangely enough, Brigadier was backed for a lot of money, as he ran in Mr Gorton's nomination, and this gentleman had backed "his nomination" expecting it to be filled by a smart bitch in Wild Geranium : she unfortunately went wrong at the last minute and her place was taken by the winner. A lucky winner for all !

The Waterloo Cup

Now comes the time that is perhaps the most memorable of all times in long-tail history, as for a few years the form of the greyhounds was of the very highest class. In the last eight left in the Cup for 1868 were Lobelia, Brigade, Cock Robin, Charming May and Master M'Grath, whilst Bab-at-the-Bowster is only outside the eight owing to having been beaten by Lobelia in the previous round. Any one of these was equal to taking a Cup in an ordinary year, and every one has left a mark that will last. In 1867 Mr Stocker nominated Lobelia owing to his picked dog, Saucebox, having gone wrong. They had been previously tried, and the little bitch (she only weighed 44 lb.) had gone so well that, when Saucebox failed him, he put Lobelia in and, what is more, backed her. Her early courses were a little unsteady, and she was dreadfully cut about in her first trial with Lord Soulis, but beat Royal Seal, a Patent dog, as she liked. The parish church bells at Southport were rung in honour of her win. From the old picture, by Armstrong, in front of me as I write, there is no getting away from the fact that she is the best-looking of the three dogs. She was by Seafoam, by Beacon—Scotland Yet, ex Lilac.

The next four years are really those of Master M'Grath—a dog that made for himself a name that, like that of Fred Archer, Bottomley and possibly Lloyd George, was known in every cottage in the kingdom, and whose photo figured alike on the walls of the tavern and the smoke-room. Everyone spoke of his merits, all worshipped at his shrine, and for those few brief years, at any rate, no one lived who did not know that the Waterloo was run at Altcar and that the hares were not dropped out of bags.

Master M'Grath, a black-and-white dog, was by Dervock ex Lady Sarah. Dervock went back in tail male line to the great King Cob, whilst Lady Sarah was by David, a combination of Sam and Senate blood.

In 1868 he started none too well, as his first course was an undecided with Belle of Scotland, but he made amends in his run-off and beat her, then Kalista, then the favourite, Brigade, and Lobelia, the 1867 winner. Lobelia had, after an undecided, beaten Bab-at-the-Bowster, who came from Scotland with a big reputation, having divided at the Scottish National Meeting and also divided the Croxteth Stakes—ninety dogs—at Altcar in the previous year.

Charming May met her brother, Cock Robin (both were by King Death out of Chloe), in the semi-final and was withdrawn in his favour, though the wisdom of this may well be doubted, as she beat him as she liked in the consequent bye which he ran. He met Master M'Grath in the final but was of no use whatever to

HOPREND, WINNER WATERLOO CUP, 1906

him, and the black-and-white had his course
all his own from the turn onwards.

The following year, 1869, was full of
interest, as Master M'Grath had won the
Brownlow Cup since his Waterloo and Bab-
at-the-Bowster had taken the Great Scarisbrick
Champion Cup (a hundred and twenty-eight
dogs), the Douglas Cup (sixty-four dogs), the
Altcar Club Cup, and had divided the Elsham
Cup (thirty-two dogs). Master M'Grath started
at 6 to 1 and Bab-at-the-Bowster at 10 to
1. Master M'Grath met Borealis, a Patent
bitch that ran up for the Purse, and led her
twelve lengths for the turn so that she looked
like a mere terrier shuffling after him. The
Master ran right into his hare and had flung
it up half dead into the air before the bitch
got up. He then met Hard Lines, whom he
led as far as he liked, but after turning his
hare he fell, and Hard Lines killed. He met
Lobelia in his fourth course and at one time
the little bitch fairly held him, but Master
M'Grath raced past her, put the hare to her,
and then the hare jumped a ditch into the
road and turned short back over a hare-bridge.
This was Master M'Grath's chance, and after
jumping into the road, level with Lobelia, he
turned the quicker and practically killed as he
landed back. Bab-at-the-Bowster had mean-
time been doing well and had run good courses

against Sir William and Ghillie Callum, whom many fancied for the Cup outright, and when the time came for Master M'Grath and Bab-at-the-Bowster to go to the slips for the final, a silence fell on that huge crowd—a silence that only those who have experienced it on the Friday of a Waterloo final on those cold, bleak Altcar plains can understand.

Scotland and Ireland were represented in the slips for a memorable Cup and ran one of the most memorable courses ever recorded.

The course was run on the farthest of the Hill House meadows, bounded by the road leading to the Withins. The crowd was on the embankment and the beaters were driving from the other side of the main road. From a perfect slip by Raper—the Wilkinson of those days—Master M'Grath began to draw out, but, in a long straight parallel to the ditch, Bab-at-the-Bowster gradually collared him and as they neared the bridge was actually leading him. This was fatal to her, as the hare turned short over the bridge and, whilst Bab had to go round, Master M'Grath slipped up on to the inside and was over first. The hare doubled right back, and then followed a long series of the quickest exchanges in which it was a case of " six of one and half-a-dozen of the other." This went on until they were nearly back at the starting-place, when Master M'Grath with a terrific effort drew out, wrenched hard and killed. Bonfires were lighted on that Friday night on the hills near Belfast to tell of the second victory of Lord Lurgan's wonderful dog. At Waterloo it created so much excitement in the bosom of at least one Irishman that, having flung away his own hat, he rushed at Lord Lurgan, plucked off his lordship's hat and flung it into the air, kicking it to the winds as it fell. This final of 1869 is handed down to history as one of the greatest of courses, never eclipsed, but possibly equalled by the final between Harmonicon and Hopsack in 1916.

In 1870 the meeting was interfered with by frost and was not started until the Wednesday following. Master M'Grath had not been seen in public since his last Cup, but was a very strong favourite at 7 to 2. He met Lady Lyons in the first round, and, to the consternation of all, it was soon seen that she was not only leading him but giving him a very severe hiding. The course ended, with Lady Lyons well in front, at the River Alt, which was still covered over with rotten ice. In following the hare the ice gave way, and it was only through the pluck of Wilson, the Irish slipper, that Master M'Grath was saved from drowning. On the following day he was in an awful state, but, though Lord Lurgan insisted that he had been poisoned, there is no doubt that he was short of work and upset by the bad going.

Bab-at-the-Bowster won three courses, but was then beaten by Cataclysm, a dog that had run up for the Plate in the previous year, and the race eventually went to Sea Cove, who beat Bendimere in the final. Bed of Stone, who won in 1872, took the Purse from a very useful dog in S. S., who was very unlucky to lose her first tie in the Cup.

This year was remarkable as being the one and only one in which an objection has to be recorded, but this was not against any one dog, but against the action of the stewards in postponing the meeting.

1871 saw Master M'Grath win his third Waterloo and run his last course in public. Starting at 10 to 1, he gave his backers many anxious moments in his first course with Wharfinger, but warmed to his work as he went along, and beat the puppy Pretender pretty easily for the final. Like Cerito and Fullerton, the other triple winners, and Coomassie and Miss Glendyne, the two dual winners, Master M'Grath was practically a failure at the Stud and died of heart disease two years after his last win.

In this year Bed of Stone, by Portland out of Imperatrice, who had won the Purse in 1870, had bad luck, as she ran three undecided courses with Bendimere, but won the Plate and took the Cup at her third attempt the following year. In the final she beat Peasant Boy—by Racing Hopfactor, a son of David, ex Placid—who filled the same berth in the next year. Bed of Stone was an extraordinary bitch that made a huge success at Stud through her single son, Bedfellow, by Contango. Amongst those behind her were Chameleon, one of the King Death — Chloe combination, who won the Purse ; and Liberty, also by King Death, who ran up for the Purse.

In the next year, 1873, Muriel won for Mr R. Jardine from Peasant Boy, the runner-up in 1872, and another of the same owner in Joan divided the Purse with Contango, afterwards to become famous as a sire, after two undecided courses.

This was Mr Warwick's last year as a judge, and his tenure of office was terminated by a regrettable outburst on the part of the crowd who, having heard rumours that he had judged a private trial of Peasant Boy, literally mobbed him when the two finalists went to the slips. Contango was, without a doubt, the best grey-hound in the race, as he was afterwards not only sire of Bedfellow, but was sire of Ptarmigan, sire of Princess Dagmar ; Paris, sire of Miss Glendyne, and Bit of Fashion, dam of Fullerton ; and Jester. He was also sire of Master Sam the

sire of Macpherson, sire of Herschel, Greater
Scot, etc., and sire of Misterton and, through
Bedfellow, of Greentick. Truly a great sire and
a credit to his parents, Cashier and that marvel,
Bab-at-the-Bowster.

In 1874 Mr Hedley was appointed judge
for the first time. Magnano, an outsider, won,
after putting Muriel out in the first round, from
Surprise. Gallant Foe was beaten in the second
round of the Cup, much to the disgust of the
crowd, and won the Plate. She was the co-
partner with Ptarmigan in the wonderful litter
Paris, Jester and Princess Dagmar, which equalled
the famous King Death—Chloe and Beacon—
Scotland Yet combinations.

In 1875 the Irish bitch, Honeymoon, won
from Corby Castle after an undecided. Sirius
started a hot favourite but was beaten in
the first round. Honeymoon, who then won
the Brownlow Cup, started a hot favourite the
following year at 11 to 2, but after beating
Warren Hastings, Handicraft and Lucetta was
beaten by her stable companion Donald, who
won from Lord Glendyne in the final. Handicraft won the Plate from Dr Richardson's
Midnight.

1877 saw the first win of that little wonder,
Coomassie, whose pedigree must ever remain
a mystery. She was by Celebrated, by Albatross
by Tullochgorum (an own brother to King

Photograph : Sporting Chronicle

HALLOW EVE, WINNER WATERLOO CUP, 1908
From a painting by Frank Paton

Death) : this much is certain, but all else is mythical.

Coomassie was a little bitch of only 44 lb. weight, fawn and white in colour and as smart as she was small. The only dog to give her any trouble in the Cup courses was Master Sam, a son of Contango, who was one of the fastest dogs of his day but a bad killer. He led Coomassie, but let her in, and putting in some good points she killed to win, and won fairly easily from Braw Lass, the favourite, in the final. The next year, starting favourite at 9 to 1, with Braw Lass at 10's, she ran disappointingly in her first two courses, but, improving as she went on, she met Zazel in the final. This bitch had been hard run and made a fair show, but killed too soon and gave Coomassie her second Cup. During the winter of 1878–1879 great hopes were entertained that Coomassie would win the 1879 Cup and rival the feats of Cerito and Master M'Grath, but she broke a small bone in her leg whilst at exercise and never ran again. This seemingly paved the way for Zazel, who started favourite, but the winner turned up in Misterton, who started at the nice price of 1000 to 6, and won, with plenty in hand, of Commerce. This dog was by Contango and was another example of that wonderful dog's capacity as a sire. After this, though he ran in the following year's Cup, Misterton did no good until he went to Stud, when he made a name equal to Contango, MacPherson and Greentick, though he never actually sired a winner or runner-up of the Cup. Probably his best offspring were Mullingar and Habeas Corpus, who were ex Gulnare II.

The race for 1879 was remarkable from the fact that the winner of the Cup, the runner-up for the Cup, and the winner of the Purse were all by Contango, and, what is more, the first two were only puppies. Another interesting point is that during the last twelve months the name of the runner-up for the Purse—Boy o' Boys— has been repeated in Lady Helen M'Calmont's dog, recently returned as the winner of the Cork Cup.

In 1880 Misterton, despite his previous year's win, was only third favourite at 13 to 1, the first and second favourites being the Earl of Haddington's pair, Haidee and Honeywood. The former of these two was beaten in the first round, and Lady Lizzie, who had been backed for "a mint of money," broke her leg after having got Decorator well beaten. Honeywood beat Wood Reeve, MacPherson, who afterwards became such a great sire, Market Day and Surpriser, and came to the slips for the final with Plunger. This was a great course, as after Honeywood had made a brilliant opening and had gone past his opponent twice he was thrown out and let Plunger up. This dog did so much work from then on to the finish that it was a near thing when the judge—Mr Hedley—gave his verdict for Honeywood. In the following year, 1881, Honeywood started a very hot favourite at 8 to 1, but was beaten in the first round by Mr Brocklebank's Bishop, who eventually got to the final, in which he was beaten by that great bitch Princess Dagmar. In his previous course Bishop had been hard run to beat Cui Bono and was badly handicapped with the bitch, who had got off lightly all through. She went away clear from the slips, took the turn, and then went past to kill and win. Princess Dagmar started at 2000 to 45, and Plunger at 18 to 1. In 1882 another outsider, Snowflight, won from an aged bitch, Hornpipe. The former got off easily all through ; the latter, on the contrary, was hard run, so that, after an undecided and a no-course in the final, Snowflight, favoured still more by a wide inside, won fairly comfortably. Snowflight started at 1000 to 15 and Hornpipe at 1000 to 20. MacPherson won the Purse from Princess Dagmar, and Debonnaire the Plate.

In 1883 Wild Mint, the property of Mr W. Osborne, brother of the more famous John Osborne, won from Snowflight, who went to the slips for the final with the bookmakers taking 3 to 1. Wild Mint was trained by Shaw of Northallerton, who had had the training of the celebrated Coomassie previously, and killed in every course she ran. The outcome of this win was a match with Mr Reilly, of Newmarket, who considered that his dog Destruction was one better. The match was for £500 a side, and was run at Haydock Park, at the March meeting of 1883, and won by Mr Osborne's bitch by two courses to one. In 1884 Mineral Water won from Greentick, later sire of Fullerton, Trough-end, Simonian and other famous winners, and afterwards won the Gosforth Gold Cup. He was beaten in the first ties for the 1885 Waterloo, which resulted in a division between Bit of Fashion and Miss Glendyne. Both bitches were by Paris—by Ptarmigan ex Gallant Foe and one of the famous litter which included Princess Dagmar. Bit of Fashion goes down to history as dam of Fullerton, and Miss Glendyne as the winner of the 1886 Waterloo and the 1888 Plate. In 1886 Miss Glendyne started at 10 to 1 for the Cup, with Penelope II. at 100 to 8, and the puppy Greater Scot at 100 to 7. The reason for Miss Glendyne's nice price was that it was well known that she had been under treatment by Mr Hutton, of London, for a broken, or misplaced, toe. Both Miss Glendyne and Penelope II. ran well, the former having beaten Greater Scot and the latter Clamour in good trials, and in the semi-finals the one ran rings round Luther and the other won from the hard-run Pinkerton. The two bitches went to the slips for the final, and Penelope II. was quickest away, but was caught by Miss Glendyne, who took the turn a length ahead. Penelope then got in for the second turn, and it was only by a terrific effort that Miss Glendyne got up to get in and kill. As Penelope was only a tiny bitch of 41 lb., it can be seen that she ran a wonderful course against a bigger and a better, and must have been one of the right sort to do it. She was by MacPherson, who sired the dividers, Greater Scot and Herschel, the following year. Miss Glendyne was, of course, everyone's favourite, but after running a grand course with Mereworth she dislocated her toe in a long course with Hermes, and though Dr Hutton, the bone-setter, was telegraphed for, he was in Paris and arrived too late, by ten minutes, to set it before she was due in the slips, with Longest Day in the second round. To travel from Paris to Altcar by special train to set a greyhound's toe may seem ridiculous, but greyhounds are grey-hounds, and more extraordinary things have been done and will, in all probability, be done again.

Greater Scot and Herschel were both trained in Mr Coke's kennel at Birkdale. In 1888 a postponement was necessary on account of the frost, and a fresh draw was made, which was unfortunate, as Herschel and Miss Glendyne were drawn together in the first round instead of being wide apart as they were in the original draw. They were slipped to a three-legged hare, and Herschel took the turn two lengths clear. Miss Glendyne then got in momentarily, but the dog went past her like a rocket to kill. After this, Herschel's course with Mahonia was poor, and, though he did well against Tullochgorum, Burnaby beat him pretty easily and went on to win the final from Colonel North's Duke MacPherson. The winner afterwards divided the Gosforth Gold Cup with Huic Halloa.

The next four years are concerned entirely with Colonel North and his wonderful dog Fullerton, who divided with his kennel mate, Troughend, in 1889 and won in 1898, 1891 and 1892—a record never equalled and never likely to be surpassed.

Fullerton was bought at the sale of Mr Dent's kennel at the Barbican for 850 guineas and Troughend at the January sale for 470 guineas. Besides these two, Colonel North ran four other dogs in the 1889 race : Miss Kitten, for whom he had paid 160 guineas ; Miss Glendyne, whom he bought for 510 guineas ; Dingwall, purchased for 255 guineas ; and Sorais. That this state of affairs is desirable in the best interests of the sport is very doubtful, but it would hardly be allowed at the present day, so matters not. Fullerton beat Dear Belle and then Blue Blood,

DENDRASPIS, WINNER WATERLOO CUP, 1909

then ran an undecided with Barbican II., but won in the run-off and then beat Sorais. Herschel had had an awful course on the Thursday afternoon, as in his fourth course he ran a hare single-handed from the Withins to Gore House Wood, and in coming back got on to two fresh hares and ran them until he lay down exhausted.

As a natural consequence, he came out stiff on the next day, and went down to Fullerton. Troughend beat, amongst others, Miss Glendyne and Burnaby and, in the semi-final, Danger Signal, and divided the Cup with Fullerton. In 1890 Fullerton started at 9 to 2 and was heavily backed, and on the first day made hacks of Plemont and Glenogle, following it up on the second day by beating Monkside and Gladiola, and went to the slips for the final with Downpour, whom he beat as easily as the . others. It is written : " Fullerton carried off the Cup in the most gallant manner and too much can hardly be written in his praise." 1891 saw him win again from Messrs Fawcetts' Faster and Faster. This latter was, at the time, one of the fastest bitches in England, but she was handicapped by being hard run all through the stake.

In this year Greentick had nineteen of his progeny in the race and sired the winners of Cup, Purse and Plate, going one better than the previous year, when he had the Cup winner and the runners-up for the Purse and Plate.

In 1892 frost, for the third time in history, caused the race to be postponed over the week-end, and Fullerton again took all before him, though in his third course, against Rhymes, he was at one period well beaten but stayed on to kill and win; and in the final with Fitz Fife, after he had run an undecided, though he led him four lengths for the turn he had to go all the way in a long course to win. Both Greentick, his sire, and Bit of Fashion, his dam, were present at Altcar on the day of the final to see his win—a win which left him with the wonderful record of three Cups and a division and twenty-three courses won on the Altcar flats. In 1893 the old dog, who had proved a failure at the Stud, was entered again and started favourite at 4 to 1, with Faster and Faster and Fine Night well backed at 100 to 15 and 10 to 1. Fitz Fife and Texture, a grand little bitch, were also amongst the runners. Fullerton won his first course with Castlemartin, but age told when he met Full Captain, and, though he led at the turn, he fell in a drain and then came down again to leave Full Captain to win comfortably. All three favourites were out of it on the second day, and the last day saw Character, Patrick Blue, Button Park, and Texture left in. Character and Button Park contested the final and the former won very nicely. Character was owned by Mr Coke, and Button Park was trained by him, so that, as in Greater Scot—Herschel's year, he had the final two.

It may not be out of place to give a list of Fullerton's performances. He was by Greentick — Bit of Fashion, weighed 65½ lb., and was whelped in 1887.

In 1888–1889 he ran up for the Haydock Derby and divided the Waterloo Cup. In 1880–1890 he won the Waterloo Cup ; 1891–1892 he was drawn after winning a course for the Newton Stakes at Haydock and won the Waterloo, and in 1892–1893 he was beaten in the second course for the Cup. In all, he won thirty-one courses and lost two, and won stakes to the value of £1910. He died in 1899 and left no progeny to carry on his name. As a matter of comparison, the great Master M'Grath won three Waterloo Cups, and won thirty-six courses and lost one, with a total of £1750 in stakes ; and Bab-at-the-Bowster, who never won a Waterloo, won sixty-two courses, lost five, and credited her owner with £1540 in winnings. Comparisons are odious, and each of the three was a great greyhound on his or her day, though taken all round on racing and Stud performances, neither equals the like of Greentick, Herschel or Misterton.

In 1894 Texture, the bitch that had run so

well the year before, started at 100 to 3, and won
from Falconer, who started favourite at 100 to 15.
She belonged to Count Stroganoff, who had
purchased her a month previously for 110
guineas at the Barbican sales. In 1895 frost
was again in evidence and the race did not
come off until 13th March, three weeks after the
advertised date. To the outsider three weeks
may mean nothing, but to the owner or trainer
of greyhounds it means a very great deal, and it
was a marvel that so many dogs were put down
so fit. Falconer was again favourite, with
Fabulous Fortune, Fair Floralie, Fortuna Favente
and Thoughtless Beauty all well backed. The
last four left in were Falconer, Fortuna Favente,
Thoughtless Beauty and Gallant. Falconer was
led and easily beaten by Fortuna Favente, and
Gallant, a puppy, was outworked by Thoughtless
Beauty, who won the final after a hard course.
She belonged to Mr Pilkington, who had
previously won with Burnaby, and was bought
by him at the Barbican for 36 guineas, and, like
the winners of the Purse and Plate, was by
Herschel—by MacPherson.

1896 was chiefly remarkable for the change it
brought in the Messrs Fawcetts' luck. Previous
to this year they had run up to Fullerton with
Faster and Faster in 1891 ; ran up to him again
with Fitz Fife in 1892 ; and were just beaten by
Thoughtless Beauty with Fortuna Favente in 1895,

and Honour just beat Fertile Field in the same year for the Purse. 1896 saw their luck change, and they registered their first win with Fabulous Fortune, by Herschel out of Fair Future, a bitch that had been bought by Wright, their trainer, from a public-house in Cumberland. He was on a visit and took a fancy to a bitch lying in front of the kitchen fire : he brought her back with him, and she became dam of the 1896 winner, and the majority of the famous " F. & F." kennel trace to her. Thoughtless Beauty was favourite at 9 to 2, Fabulous Fortune next in demand at 5 to 1, and Fortuna Favente and Gallant well backed at 100 to 11 and 10 to 1. Fabulous Fortune went well in all his courses, beating Stipplefield, Reception, High Dappley Moor, Utopia and, in the final, the Irish dog Wolf Hill, who had beaten Thoughtless Beauty in the previous round. He was one of perhaps the most famous litter of all time, as he was litter brother to Faber Fortunæ, First Fortune, Fortuna Favente and Fortune's Favourite, who were all big winners.

In 1897 Gallant, who had been in the last four in 1895 and runner-up for the Plate in 1896, won from Five by Tricks. Fabulous Fortune started favourite at 4 to 1, a short price when it is remembered what has to be done to win ; Five by Tricks was at 11 to 1, and Gallant was on offer at 50 to 1, a price at which his owner backed him to win £11,000. The last four left in were Five by Tricks, Fabulous Fortune, Gallant and Black Veil. Five by Tricks was being led by Fabulous Fortune when the latter steadied himself and let Five by Tricks in for a long sequence, which was never wiped off, even though Fabulous Fortune killed. Gallant was led by Black Veil, but she brought the hare too far round and in consequence let Gallant in, when he did the rest of the work, and killed to win. Gallant then beat Five by Tricks fairly comfortably. Though not by any means a brilliant greyhound, he has left a name at Stud, as has also another runner in this year, Under the Globe, who won the Plate.

The next year was another very ordinary one, and Mr Hardy supplied the winner in Wild Night, whom he had bought with Wet Day, Five by Tricks and Wintry Weather for £800. The betting after the draw was of the old-time variety, as Gallant was backed to win £10,000 at 18 to 1 ; Wet Day the same amount at 100 to 7 ; Wild Night £14,000 at 33 to 1 ; Five by Tricks £8000, and Under the Globe £6000 at 200 to 11. Some betting, as things go nowadays! Five by Tricks was badly beaten in the first round, and Gallant, now in his fourth season, got no further than the second round ; whilst Under the Globe, after beating Wilful Maid, went down to Wild Night on the second day, and Wet Day did the same at the hands of Lang Syne. Wild Night had been running well and made many supporters by her win over Under the Globe, and, after beating Chock in the semi-final, she started favourite, at 6 to 4 on, for the final with Lang Syne. This dog went to the slips very lame, and Mr Hardy's bitch won easily. Though not a great bitch, Wild Night was marvellous in her quickness of scoring, and a wonderful killer. Peregrine Pickle, who beat Gallant, was considered by many to be a long way the best dog in the race, but unfortunately broke a toe and had to be withdrawn. Peregrine Pickle was winter favourite for the 1899 Cup, but at the eleventh hour his toe gave way again and he went out to 100 to 8, with Real Emperor and Faber Fortunæ in better demand at 100 to 12. By the time the stake had been reduced to sixteen, Wild Night, Lang Syne and Chock, who had been in 1898's last four, were out, and the Duke of Leeds' puppy Lapal was going as well as anything, and Faber Fortunæ, going like a puppy, was very well in and after the first day's running was a hot favourite at 3 to 1, but was well beaten by Black Fury, and Genetive, after beating Hackler, went down to Lapal, who had previously beaten Father o' Fire in a grand course.

The last four left in were George Tincler, Hesper, Black Fury and Lapal. Lapal met

Hesper, and the Duke of Leeds' puppy not only led her by three lengths but gave no chance away in the work that followed. Black Fury led George Tincler two lengths and never gave a point away, beating him in the most decisive manner. He started for the final with the ring taking 9 to 4, and just got up for the turn after a great race. He wrenched thrice and then let Lapal in to kill and lose. This Cup was of more than its usual interest, as there were two Australian dogs running, Bogan and Tarana's Pride, but though they came with big reputations they did no better than a similar importation in Coomassie's year, and neither survived the first round.

The dawn of another century was unfortunate in that it witnessed one of those outbursts of excessive zeal which makes one wonder where the Liverpool Watch Committee are drawn from. Just prior to the draw and usual banquet taking place, it was officially announced that, in consequence of the action of the police, under orders of the Watch Committee, no betting would be permitted ; in other words, the customary calling over of the card after the draw would be prohibited. In consequence, no draw or banquet took place, and the card was called over the following morning, whilst waiting for the frost to clear, at Hill House. Black Fury and Mister O'Shea shared equal favouritism at 10 to 1, with

Photograph: Sport and General

WINNING NUMBER, WINNER WATERLOO CUP, 1915

Father o' Fire and Peregrine Pickle backed at
100 to 7. All the 1899 last four went down in
the first round. Black Fury, with odds of 5
to 1 betted on him, was led and well beaten.
Peregrine Pickle made no show at all against
Cherry Whiskey, and Mister O'Shea and Lapal
were very disappointing. Mrs Grundy had
been running well, but found one too good in
Cherry Whiskey, who in turn went down to
Hawthorn VI. Lavishly Clothed beat Get
Hold in easy fashion after being allowed to
remain in subsequent to an undecided with
Countess Udston. The last four were Fearless
Footsteps, Hawthorn VI., Lavishly Clothed
and Prince Falcon, and Fearless Footsteps and
Lavishly Clothed went to the slips for the final
with odds of 9 to 4 on the former, who led
two lengths in the run-up. Lavishly Clothed
then got in and kept there until well in front,
but then Fearless Footsteps in again for four
strong drives and a kill to win. Lavishly
Clothed was the third run-up for the Duke of
Leeds in three successive years, Lapal in 1899
and Lang Syne in 1898 being the other two.

Fearless Footsteps was by Fabulous Fortune
ex Fille de Feu, so combined the best of the
MacPherson and Greentick blood.

1901 saw the banquet and draw transferred
to the Exchange Hotel, and the crack puppy
Farndon Ferry installed favourite at 9 to 1,

with his two kennel companions, Fearless Footsteps and Father o' Fire next in demand at 100 to 9. All three survived the first round, in which only seventeen of the thirty-two favourites won. Then Father o' Fire went down to Lady Husheen, and Farndon Ferry had all his work cut out to beat Pincher, who at the start held him, and Fearless Footsteps beat Brokerage. On the second day Garbitas ran a fine course with Border Song and, after being in a losing balance, piled up the points to win. Farndon Ferry had no difficulty in beating Public Life, and Fearless Footsteps, though outpaced all through the course, beat Guid Wife by close working and then beat Rare Luck just as easily. The last four in were Cleughbrae, Lady Husheen and the two F.'s. The former two had been run to death, and Cleughbrae in beating Lady Husheen got another gruelling. Fearless Footsteps beat Farndon Ferry after leading him a length, though there are many who say that she was " funny tempered " and the puppy was afraid to pass her. In the final Fearless Footsteps, with odds of 5 to 2 asked for, won as she liked from the distressed Cleughbrae, whose first appearance in public it was. He was by Under the Globe ex Tiny Polly—one of the Herschel —Thetis combination. Farndon Ferry started favourite the following year at 10 to 1, and he, Wartnaby, Blackheath and Grafter were the last four in. Farndon Ferry beat Grafter and Wartnaby raced past Blackheath and killed to win. For the final, Farndon Ferry was favourite with 2 to 1 asked for, and led Wartnaby for the turn and the next two, when Wartnaby got his chance, rattling his hare about in telling fashion until, by bad luck, the hare broke back to Farndon Ferry, who killed and won luckily. In the course of his progress to the final Wartnaby's hardest course was with Garbitas. The pair mated together later produced Heavy Weapon, the 1910 winner and sire of Harmonicon, the 1916 winner.

In 1903 the Messrs Fawcett took their fifth Cup, which, for the first year, was actually a Cup presented by Lord Sefton in addition to the " monkey " the winning owner makes. Farndon Ferry was favourite at 7 to 1, with his kennel companion Father Flint at 100 to 6 and Paracelsus at 100 to 8. The last four left in were Paracelsus—Mr Pilkington's third string—Handsome Creole, Farndon Ferry and Father Flint. Paracelsus just beat Handsome Creole, but Farndon Ferry made no show against his kennel mate, being well led to the hare and then outworked. In the final there was a great course, as Paracelsus only just got in front for the turn, after a neck-and-neck run-up, then Father Flint did some good work for three drives and let

Paracelsus in for three quick wrenches and an all too quick kill on which he lost.

Father Flint was by Fiery Furnace ex Fanny Faithful, and Paracelsus was one of the Under the Globe—Thoughtless Beauty litter. Other good dogs in the race were Cheers—sire of Fortuna II. dam of Lusory—Prince Charming, Agile Spurt, all of whom have left names behind them.

The first day in 1904 was an awful one for the favourites, as such fancies as Fearsome Flight, Prince Plausible, Prince Charming, Pistol II., Militant and others all went down, and on the second day Fecht Fair put " paid " to Paracelsus. This left Fecht Fair, a puppy, by Fiery Furnace—Fearless Footsteps, Minchmuir, Haughton Ferry and Homfray in the last four, and their supposed chances can be estimated by the fact that at long odds on the night of the draw their prices were, respectively, 1000 to 30, 1000 to 20, 1000 to 10 and 1000 to 5. Homfray had all the luck of a bad slip in beating Fecht Fair, and Minchmuir was all out to beat Haughton Ferry. Homfray won the final for Mr Herbert, who had bought him at the Barbican for five guineas less than a year before.

Until a fortnight previous to the race there was no intention of running him, when a nomination was applied for " for fun," with the result described. A great win for one of the "little men," as Mr Herbert had only three greyhounds in this kennel.

Pistol II., at his third attempt, and starting at the nice price of 100 to 1, took the 1905 Cup from Prince Plausible, with Mandini and Minchmuir beaten in the semi-finals. All through the stake the favourites had come down, one after another, and odds were laid on Prince Plausible for the final, only to go down in what seemed to be the usual way. Pistol II. had been at Stud before running, which may have improved him.

In 1906 another really good dog in Hoprend won at last, giving Mr Hardy his second Cup. The year was a wonderful one in many ways, as besides Hoprend there are names which the present-day coursing man reverences. Formula was one, beaten in the first round by Hoprend; then Mandini, beaten by another good one in Dividend Deferred in the semi-finals, has left his mark as a sire, and Parson Parkes is another name looked for in the puppies' pedigrees. The final was one of the finest ever seen at Altcar, as from a perfect slip Hoprend just led for the turn and second and then let Dividend Deferred in for a nice sequence, the white dog sticking to his work like a real good one. Then Hoprend replaced him, only to lose his hare in attempting to kill, and being replaced, in turn, by the white. So the course went on, with six for one and half-a-dozen for the other, until Hoprend got in to kill and just win from a really great dog.

The next two years saw the brother and sister of Formula take the Cup, in 1907 Long Span, and in 1908 Hallow Eve. All three were by Pateley Bridge out of Forest Fairy and all three have left names not likely to be forgotten.

In 1907 Formula ran again but went down to Such a Mark, and Hallow Eve, after beating Lottery, met one too good in Hidden Career, who in turn was beaten by Such a Mark. Long Span beat Crash, Father Prout and Little Mercury before meeting Hoprend, whom he led three lengths and outworked. Glenbridge and Long Span met in the final after beating Such a Mark and Platonic respectively, but Long Span never gave a point away and won as he liked. For the 1908 event, Long Span started favourite at 7 to 2, but was beaten by his sister Hallow Eve, who started at 66 to 1, in the semi-final, and had previously well outworked Dendraspis. Odds of 11 to 2 were laid on Long Span, and though he led four lengths to the hare he did nothing more, and once again a really clever, genuine bitch beat a faster dog. For the final she went to the slips with Silhouette, who had outworked Bachelor's Acre, and though being led in the run-up she won absolutely by work and sheer grit, for Mr Hulton, who had paid 225 guineas for her as a sapling.

1909 saw Dendraspis register the first win for the popular brothers, Messrs S. M. and J. E. Dennis. Long Span was again favourite at 3 to 1, but was put out in the first ties by Royal Crest, who in turn was beaten by Such a Sell, who went to the slips for the final with Dendraspis, who had beaten Second Barrel, the conqueror of Heavy Weapon, in the semi-final. Dendraspis just got the turn and, after Such a Sell had to run up a sequence, got up again to kill and win. There were some good dogs behind the winner in Writ, Broad Arrow, Heavy Weapon, etc.

1910 saw Long Span, for the fourth time, favourite at 7 to 1, with Heavy Weapon well backed at 10 to 1. Long Span got as far as the second round, but Heavy Weapon was too good for him. Full Steam beat Beaded Brow and then Calabash in the semi-final, but was so hard run that he was incapable of going to the slips for the final, so that the Cup, for the first time on record, was awarded without a race to Heavy Weapon, afterwards to be famous as the sire of Harmonicon and the Golden trio : Sun, Sabre and Signet.

Sir R. W. R. Jardine was not long in replacing Long Span, for in 1911 he ran the puppy Jabberwock, who started at 50 to 1 and took another Cup for the famous Castlemilk kennels. This was another case of favourites going down all the time, as the three others of the last four in were Mandate, Raby Bachelor, both of whom were at 100 to 1 on the night of the draw, and Silk and Scarlet, against whose chance 40 to 1 was freely offered. All four were puppies, two of the four being Scotch and two English. Silk and Scarlet beat Mandate after leading him two lengths and then outworking him, and Jabberwock also led Raby Bachelor two lengths and then let the latter in to kill and lose. In the final, Silk and Scarlet led a couple of lengths to the hare, took the turn and the second, but then let Jabberwock in. This dog ran up a long sequence and when the hare came down in a ditch was an easy winner.

He was by Bachelor's Acre, by Farndon Ferry — Filagree, ex Forrester's Favour, by Under the Globe — Fantine. Mr Stollery's puppy, Sylph, was very unlucky to be beaten in a fluky course in her first round. Her litter brother, Saracen, was favourite in 1912 at 15 to 2. Jabberwock was beaten in the first round by Hustings, and Harrow Wanderer was beaten in the second round by Distingué. Then Tide Time, a puppy, was too good for Saracen, and Such a Sell beat Mandate. The last four in were Adversary, Hyson, Tide Time and Hidden Smoke, whose prices at the draw were 40 to 1 either of the three former and 100 to 1 against

HONEYMAN AND FIGHTING FORCE IN THE SLIPS FOR THE 1920 FINAL

the latter. Tide Time beat Hyson and Adversary beat Hidden Smoke.

For the final, Tide Time beat Adversary after a great course. He belonged to Mr Townshend, whose first season's coursing it was and who had bought him for 25 guineas at the Barbican sale. This was Mr Mugliston's first season as Waterloo Secretary and Mr Walker's first as Judge, so that it can well be called a novice year.

Tide Time started a sound favourite the next year at 9 to 1, with Broadmoor at 10's and Hung Well and Hirundo at 100 to 8, Saracen at 100 to 6 and Distingué at 20 to 1. Adversary, last year's runner-up, came down in the first round, but Patent, Broadmoor, Rapid Doctor and Distingué all won courses, and Tide Time beat the smart puppy Clerical Error all one way. Saracen beat Short Circuit and Half Nelson lost Harrow Wanderer. In the second round Mandate met a better, Distingué beat Patent, Corsica beat Half Nelson, and Huldee beat Klip River.

Hung Well just beat Tide Time after a great course in the next round, and Saracen went down to Fellow from Wales. The last four were Hung Well, Dancing Dervish, Fellow from Wales and Huldee. Hung Well beat Dancing Dervish and Huldee ran a bye, as Fellow from Wales was drawn, and got a

terrible doing down, which gave Hung Well
an easy win in the final course and registered
Mr Hill Wood's second Cup in three years.

1914 was reckoned one of the most open years
of all time, and Tide Time, the 1912 winner,
was favourite at 100 to 14 ; next came Distingué
at 8 to 1, then Husky Whisper at 9 to 1 and
Hung Well at 100 to 6, with Dilwyn at 20's
offered. An international character was introduced, as there were two Australian-bred greyhounds and a Russian dog in the stake. This
latter was Chekan, who beat Mr Hardy's
Hoprend puppy, Hopsack, in the first round
pointless. The Australian Captain Large beat
Fiesole, and Once Australia beat Silviana Again.
Tide Time had a very hard run to beat the
puppy Hydra, who held him all through, and
Hung Well came down to a better dog in
Babylon, who led in the run-up, came round on
the outer circle and, after giving Hung Well his
chance, went in again to kill and win. Husky
Whisper II. beat Legal Letter in a weak course
that should have been an undecided, and Silk
and Scarlet beat the plodder Enoch. In the
second round Distingué beat the Russian dog
" all ends up," and Coming Hero beat Captain
Wood after a pretty trial, and Tide Time put an
end to Once Australia. The last four in were
Tide Time, Leucoryx, Distingué and Dilwyn.
Dilwyn beat Distingué all one way and Tide

Time lost to a better dog in Leucoryx. In the final it was no secret that Leucoryx was lame, and Dilwyn won as she liked with odds of 2 to 1 laid on her. In Leucoryx the Duke of Leeds owned his fourth runner-up for the Cup, the others being Lapal, Lang Syne and Lavishly Clothed. Once Australia took the Plate for Mr Oscar Asche.

In 1915 Hopsack was favourite at 10 to 1; then came Harmonicon at 100 to 9, Harrogate Waters at 100 to 6 and Winning Number at 100 to 5. Legal Letter, My Mascot, Lusory, Enoch, Martini and Hopsack all came down in the first round, whilst the ties saw Babylon, Full Speed, False Forecast, Captain Large, Harmonicon and Tomahawk deleted. The last four were Winning Number, Nip Near—a 200 to 1 shot—Happy Challenge and Hadfield still in. The finalists were Winning Number and Happy Challenge, the former giving nothing away except the kill. This was Sir Thomas Dewar's first attempt at the Cup, and Winning Number was bought by him at the Barbican for 280 guineas.

1916 saw the last Waterloo run prior to its abandonment owing to the war. Harmonicon was favourite at 1000 to 140 and Hopsack came next at 8 to 1, which was exceptional picking, considering that these two were the finalists. The other two in the last four were Rataine, whose price at the draw was 1000 to 15, and Minstrel Coon at the nice price of 1000 to 4.

Lord Protector, the Irish hope, went well in his early courses, but was working too wide for Waterloo and came down to the Irish puppy Minstrel Coon. Rataine ran well all through and was a really fast bitch, giving nothing away. Minstrel Coon was drawn lame in the semi-finals, giving Hopsack a bye, which was a short one. Harmonicon beat Rataine all one way and, after a great course, beat Hopsack for the final. In the opinion of many, this was the finest Waterloo final since Master M'Grath beat Bab-at-the-Bowster, as it was six for one and half-a-dozen for the other all the time, and the better plucked dog won. Harmonicon was sold to Mr Gorey in 1917 for 600 guineas and now stands at Stud in Ireland.

In 1917, 1918 and 1919 the Waterloo Cup was abandoned owing to the stress of the European War, and 'twas not until 1920 that coursers from all over the country again assembled at Altcar. The war had, as in every sport, had its effect on coursing, and there was no very firm favourite for the big event. Staff Job and Derringer held pride of place at 1000 to 90, but, whilst the former reached the last four, the latter went down in the first round to A, a fast puppy by Babylon, who also went on to the semi-finals. Mornington and Magog, two of Hopsack's produce, had come north with great reputations, and the former well beat Glencourt II., but then was unluckily

SHOWING EXACT POINT AT WHICH HONEYMAN TURNED OFF TO LET
FIGHTING FORCE WIN THE 1920 WATERLOO CUP

beaten by Halston, whilst this latter found one all too good for him in Hailfellow. The Australian dog, only just out of quarantine, Boy Ben, ran two great courses against Roving Stranger and Holystone; then beat H. S. One and was unlucky to be beaten by Fighting Force, as, after leading him a long way, he ran wide on the slippery surface and never got in again. Honeyman had all through been running brilliant courses, and though, like Fighting Force, on the slow side, made friends each time. These two, with the puppies Staff Job and A, made up the final quartet. Staff Job was too uncertain all through. Some of his courses were brilliant, others completely the reverse, and he was very lucky to get so far as he did. A, again, was fast but not too close a worker, and it was no surprise to me to see Fighting Force and Honeyman go to the slips for the final — and what a final! From a great slip they raced locked together for a long way, and then Honeyman gradually drew out and scored the turn by a full length and went on for a nice sequence when, the hare turning towards the crowd, he stopped dead and then, turning off at a tangent, raced away in the opposite direction, leaving Fighting Force to go on and do the rest to win Honeyman's Waterloo. Standing on the bank it was an extraordinary sight to watch, and one can only regret that the best dog did not win. A lot of nonsense was

The Greyhound & Coursing

written with reference to Honeyman " turning it up," as no dog could have run the courses he ran right through the stake and yet be bad plucked, and the only possible explanation is that he was scared at the crowd, which is a very different thing.

Fighting Force, the winner, worked well all through but was not, or is not, a brilliant dog, and won entirely on work. He was the property of Mr S. Beers, who bought him just prior to the meeting from Miss Fawcett. An extraordinary coincidence in connection with the race was the " code " words printed on each day's official card. On the first day it was " The Navy," on the second " The Army " and on the third " The R.A.F."—surely a tip, if ever one was given, for the winner :

SHOW THIS SIDE.

THE NAVY

1st. **DAY.**   COMPLIMENTARY

Waterloo Coursing Meeting
1920.

SHOW THIS SIDE.

THE ARMY

2nd. **DAY.**   COMPLIMENTARY

Waterloo Coursing Meeting
1920.

SHOW THIS SIDE.

THE R.A.F.

3rd. **DAY.**   COMPLIMENTARY

Waterloo Coursing Meeting
1920.

An " official tip " for the Waterloo Cup.—The cards for the three days showed three arms of the service, and the winning dog was Fighting Force !

78

The Waterloo Cup

Nimble Naiad beat Derringer in the final of the Purse, and Jack-in-Office beat Golden Sunray for the Plate.

If 1920 was a memorable year, 1921 was a super-memorable one. From Christmas onwards there were rumours concerning the judge. During the war the Withins had been under plough and was, in the opinion of the Waterloo management, not yet fit to ride over. It was therefore proposed that the first day's judging should be undertaken from a ladder. This led to a lot of correspondence in the papers, and Mr Walker, who had been elected to judge, resigned, his place being filled by Mr Mulcaster, who must be congratulated on the pluck he showed in taking on such a task in his initial effort.

At the draw, Guards Brigade at 1000 to 70, Staff Job at 1000 to 30, Boy Ben at 1000 to 40, Shortcoming at 1000 to 50, Irish Steeple at the same price, Sir Berkeley at 1000 to 60 and Jassiona at 1000 to 60 were in the most demand.

On the first day, at the Withins, the first point of interest was "the ladder," which was soon recognised as an enlarged ladder something after the style of that used at tennis matches. The judging was excellent, and throughout the day Mr Mulcaster's decisions were all that could be desired. In the first round, favourites were soon going down, as in the very first course Staff Job beat Guards Brigade. Then soon afterwards

Hailfellow beat Hawklike, who came from Ireland with a great reputation, and Thalia put a quick "paid" to Sir Berkeley, an overrated puppy. In the second round Boy Ben, who did not run the dog he was in 1920, went down to Ditton Dancer; Jemadar was of no use to Denny; Woodcut beat Jimmy the I., and Thalia beat Laurel Leaf.

Shortcoming and Jassiona with the puppy Thalia were running great courses. The former beat Gemina and Honest Solicitor, Jassiona beat Littleton Mars and Diapason, and Thalia beat Sir Berkeley and Laurel Leaf.

On the second day, at Lydiate, with the judge once more in the saddle, Matrimony running a great dog beat Staff Job in the first course. Then Hailfellow, Mr Hearn's second string, put "paid" to Dry Goods. Shortcoming beat Woodcut, and Irish Steeple, one of the fastest dogs Ireland has produced for years, ran away from Belvidere. In the fourth round Hailfellow, Jassiona, Shortcoming and Thalia stood their ground, and at the call-over in the evening Jassiona was favourite at 2 to 1, with Shortcoming a point easier at 5 to 2, Hailfellow at 3 to 1 and Thalia at 5 to 1.

The third day was one of sensations. In the first place, fog prevented a start being made until after noon, and then soon after, during the course between Jimmy the I. and Cannobie Lee in the second round of the Plate, Mr Mulcaster's horse put his foot in a hole and threw his rider with such force that he was unable to continue judging, and Mr Hector Clarke stepped into the breach and judged the remaining courses. Thus two judges actually judged the Waterloo Cup, a record which it is hoped will not, for similar reasons, be repeated.

Jassiona beat Hailfellow and Shortcoming accounted for Thalia, and then the next sensation arose, as just before the final the betting, in which Jassiona was favourite, veered round, and a rumour, unfortunately a fact, went about that Jassiona was lame.

This was obvious when the pair went down for the final, and though Jassiona did her best, Shortcoming won a great course and credited Lord Sefton with his first Waterloo—a fitting termination to the history of the Waterloo Cup to date, as Lord Molyneux won the first and Lord Sefton the last. No name is more closely connected with coursing, no family has done more for the sport and no single man is more popular than the present holder of the title.

Shortcoming is a litter sister to Staff Job, by Staff Officer ex Just Coming, and was off her food throughout the meeting, being so bad at one time that there was a possibility of her having to be withdrawn.

Guards Brigade beat Fighting Force for the final of the Purse, and Diapason beat January in the Plate.

III

Applied Anatomy and Physiology

IN a book of this description—eminently practical, I hope—it is neither necessary nor desirable to go into the details of anatomy or physiology ; nevertheless there are points of interest in both that must be mentioned. In regard to anatomy, most of the points of interest can be better understood by reference to the Plate than they would be from a lengthy description.

Under cover of the muscles shown in the Plate there is an important muscle, the serratus ventralis, situated on each side of the thorax— or lung space. This muscle arises from the last five neck vertebræ and the first eight ribs and is inserted into the upper part of the under surface of the scapula or shoulder blade. The dog is swung anteriorly by this muscle, which acts as a kind of sling in which the dog's body is suspended between his fore legs. The rest of the muscles comprising those of the shoulder and leg are concerned in propelling the body forwards in the swing and actually act, with the bones, as carriers for it. To go into the details of their origin and attachment is unnecessary, as from the Plate can be seen at a glance where they are situated and so where massage must be applied in order to encourage their action.

The physiological part cannot be explained quite so simply. When a muscle contracts, to produce movement, it becomes shorter and thicker; its extensibility is increased, its elasticity diminished, its temperature rises and an increased amount of oxygen is extracted from the blood and a corresponding amount of waste product, such as carbonic acid, is given off. This latter is, at the moment, the important point and, for it to be understood, a word must be written about the circulatory system. The heart of the dog consists of four chambers designated, respectively, the right auricle, the right ventricle, the left auricle and the left ventricle. Now when a muscle contracts the carbonic acid passes into the blood-stream and is then carried to the right auricle, from which it is passed to the right ventricle. The function of the right ventricle is to pump the blood through the lung arteries—the pulmonary arteries—into the smaller capillaries of the lungs. Here an interchange takes place: the carbonic acid unites with a certain amount of the oxygen from the air circulating in the lungs, and is given off as carbonic acid gas or carbon dioxide, whilst the blood, to replace it, takes up still more oxygen and returns with it to the left auricle. From here it passes to the left ventricle, from whence it is pumped through the large arteries, the small arteries and the arterioles to the capillaries of the muscles and body.

The more rapidly the muscle contracts, the more carbonic acid there is produced. Now the respiratory system is governed by a centre in the brain which is an automatic one, acquiring its energy from nutrition and from oxygen supplied to it by the blood, but it exhibits a peculiar irritability to carbonic acid and directly the pressure of this gas rises above a certain point in the blood the respiratory centre is so stimulated that the respiratory movements are increased in depth, thus increasing the space of lung in which the interchange of gases takes place.

From this brief review it can be seen that the muscles of a greyhound (or, for that matter, any living thing) are in close connection with the heart, the lungs, and the brain and nervous system. All these huge systems must be in perfect co-ordination for the muscle to do its work properly and accurately. Any defect in either one of them will throw the whole circuit out and the object of training must therefore be, not only to increase the power and strength of the muscles, but to tone up and quicken the working of the circulatory, the respiratory and

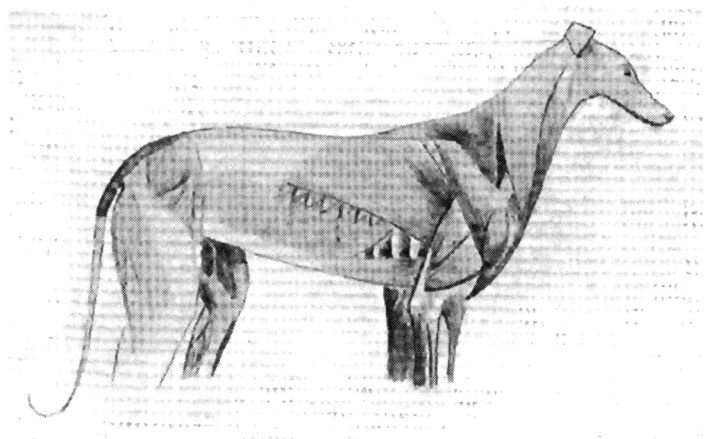

The Muscles of a Greyhound

the nervous system to work methodically and accurately.

When a muscle is at rest its reaction is alkaline, but after it has contracted and kept on contracting for a time it becomes acid, due to the formation of carbonic acid and another acid, —sarcolactic acid ; and if the contractions are continued, in course of time all the available oxygen becomes used up and these two products become formed in excess, and the condition known as fatigue sets in. This is due entirely to a too greatly increased production of carbonic acid without a corresponding increase of oxygen. The capacity of the lungs is limited, the frequency of the respirations and the heart can only be increased to a certain extent, and in consequence there comes a time when the output of waste products exceeds the intake of pure products and the whole system gives way to fatigue, which if continued would terminate in asphyxia and death due to poisoning by carbonic acid gas.

In the case of a greyhound, he is said to be "dead beat" and is much distressed. His eyes protrude, the whites are bloodshot, and the lips are blue. Gradually, as he is rested, the muscles stop contracting, no more carbonic acid gas or sarcolactic acid is formed, and the intake of oxygen gradually counterbalances the excess of these substances that are present, then replaces them ; the muscles return to normal, the waste products have been eliminated and the dog is relieved.

The old practice in cases of this description was to relieve the excess of carbonic acid by the withdrawal of blood, but the more obvious and up-to-date method would surely be the administration of oxygen. In the case of great distress, I think it will be agreed that the administration of this gas is justifiable and can be no more designated as "dope" than the administration of port wine or brandy.

These are, I think, the chief points in the anatomy and physiology of the dog that are of use to owners and trainers and they will, if necessary, be enlarged upon under the headings of the various diseases.

IV

The Breeding of Greyhounds

BEFORE embarking on the breeding of any kind of stock it is absolutely necessary for the breeder to have some idea of the basic principles of the subject. Scientific breeding is to-day enshrouded in a great many theories, but there is a certain number of proved facts and these must be understood.

In the first place, all diseases, faults and capabilities of all living matter can be divided into two great categories depending entirely as to whether they are

(1) Inborn, or
(2) Acquired.

To understand these two terms it is necessary to look for a minute at another point. The origin of all forms of life lies in what is known as the living " cell," and the most primitive of animals consist in their entirety of one single cell. As the forms of life rise above this level, more and more cells are added and the animal becomes a multicellular organism. Now the cells of which it is composed are of two main kinds : the germ, or birth, cells, and the somatic, or body, cells. The first of these, the germ cells, are the most important and are the result of the fertilisation of one germinal cell, the ovum, from one parent by another germinal cell, the sperm, from the other parent, and by division they form similar germinal cells in the female ova and in the male sperms which in their turn are fertilised and form further germinal cells. Thus there is continuity of the germ cells, which are in a real sense immortal. These cells are the true ITS, the bearers of the heredity of the individual, and pass on from generation to generation.

The second group of cells—the somatic cells —are essentially protective or covering cells. In the most primitive animals, the unicellular, they are probably represented by the cell mass which surrounds and protects the nucleus, the real germinal centre, but in the higher animals they are highly differentiated, always with the idea of protection and use, into muscle cells, bone cells, skin cells, etc. These cells are increased by division but never by conjugation, hence show no sign of continuity, and begin and end as protective coverings to their particular germinal cells.

Besides being different in function, these two classes of cells are dissimilar in another way. As is well known, no growth or other form of

" vital " activity ever occurs except as a reaction
to some appropriate kind of stimulus. Stimuli
are briefly—or better, broadly—of three main
kinds : nutriment, use and injury. Now the
germinal cells develop under the stimulus of
nourishment, or nutriment, but, though this
is of course essential, the main factors which
regulate the growth of the somatic cells are the
stimuli of use and injury.

These points are important for the under-
standing of the subjects of particular interest to
live-stock breeders—viz. the Inborn and Acquired
Diseases, Faults or Virtues of their stock. An
inborn disease, fault or virtue is one which
affects the germinal cells and which is produced
under the stimulus of nutriment ; whereas an
acquired disease, fault or virtue is one which
affects the somatic or body cells and which is
produced under the stimuli of use and injury.
It can thus be seen that the inborn and the
acquired diseases, faults or virtues are in two
entirely and absolutely different categories.
The " inborn " affects the germinal cells and so
is continuous and hereditable ; the " acquired "
affects the somatic cells and so is not continuous
and cannot be transmitted. Take an example :
Rickets is a disease of the bony skeleton—the
somatic cells—due to insufficiency of a food factor, unhealthy surroundings, etc. It is, therefore,
an acquired disease and cannot be transmitted ;

whereas hare-lip of the human being is due to an arrest in the development of the fœtus, whilst in utero, and so is a disease—or rather a temporary arrest of work—of the germinal cells, is inborn, produced under the stimulus, or lack of it, of nutriment, and is most certainly transmittable.

If this is understood and applied to the greyhound, it will at once be seen that the main essentials of a good greyhound—speed, stamina and working powers—are all inborn characteristics and are therefore inherited. By training, feeding, etcetera, they may be increased up to a certain *predestined* point, but beyond that point it is impossible for them to be improved.

This explains the points, faults or diseases that are hereditary and so transmittable, but when one turns to the manner in which they are transmitted the question becomes much more difficult to answer.

Mendel, as is well known, propounded a theory, based on his experiments with sweet-peas, by which he explained the transference of single, and opposite, characters from the parent stock to succeeding generations. Now in the greyhound all the inherited characters are dependent on a combination of many factors. Speed, for example, depends not only upon the skeletal conformation of the dog, but also upon the composition of the muscles working over i and the motor-nerve force stimulating them to action. The complexity of the co-ordinating characters is such that—at any rate for the moment — any explanation on the Mendelian hypothesis is out of the question.

A great deal of very valuable and original work has been done on the question of speed and stamina, in relation to the racehorse, by "Mankato" of *The Sporting Chronicle*, and in a recent letter from him he suggested that Galton's Law might be applicable to greyhounds in the same way as he had found it work out in relation to horses. This law presupposes that the two parents contribute, between them, on the average half of each inherited faculty, each of them contributing one quarter. The four grandparents contribute between them one-fourth, or each of them one-sixteenth. The eight great-grandparents contribute one-eighth, or each of them one-sixty-fourth ; and so on : the whole of the inheritance of the individual equalling the sum of the series.

Now, as "Mankato" writes, "In order to apply Galton's Law with any chance of success one should be in the possession of very accurate data," and this is exactly what we in the coursing world find impossible to obtain. All idea of the speed, stamina or pluck of the greyhound is comparative. The courses are of uncertain length and duration, and the distances covered and the speed at which they are covered are unknown.

Scientifically speaking, neither Mendelism nor Galton's Law can be applied, but, practically speaking, there are results known that work out, when taken as a whole, very much in accordance with them.

Mendel, for example, in his experiments with sweet-peas, interbred a tall and a short variety and got a hybrid generation. He then interbred these hybrids and found that he obtained 75 per cent. tall plants and 25 per cent. dwarf plants. These small plants were again interbred and produced nothing but small plants ; but the 75 per cent. of tall plants when interbred produced two kinds : (1) a mixed collection of talls and dwarfs ; (2) nothing but talls—the ratio of (1) to (2) being as 2 to 1. In this way he found that by breeding between two hybrids— or intermediates—the result was 25 per cent. tall, 50 per cent. mixed and 25 per cent. dwarf. The talls were proved to be dominant and the dwarfs recessive, and each, when bred *inter se*, bred true ; whereas the mixed, when interbred, produced the same formula of 25 per cent. tall, or pure dominants ; 50 per cent. mixed, or impure dominants ; and 25 per cent. dwarf, or pure recessives.

Now, for the sake of simplicity, take the letters DD to represent pure dominants, RR to represent pure recessives, and DR to represent intermediates or, in Mendel's terminology, impure dominants. The result of the union of two DR's would work out as follows :—

$$DR \times DR = 1 \ DD, \ 2 \ DR, \ 1 \ RR$$

— that is to say, there would be one pure dominant to every three others.

If one glances through the lists of sires in old *Greyhound Stud Books*, it will be noted that from time to time a sire crops up which, seemingly, throws winners no matter what bitch he is mated with. Misterton did this, Greentick was the same, and now Lusory is following in their footsteps.

Starting with the supposition that the parents of Lusory, for example, were both impure dominants and that the average greyhound litter is four, then it is surely probable, even if not proved scientifically, that Lusory was the pure dominant—the DD—of his litter. Now take the possible matings and their results :

> DD × DD equals all DD
> DD × DR equals ½ DD, ½ DR
> DD × RR equals all DR

This means that, taking the average number in the litter to be four, there would be in the three litters from a DD sire : six DD puppies and six DR puppies, with an entire absence of RR—or pure recessive—puppies.

Now take a stud dog who is an impure

dominant — DR — and the results would work out as follows :—

$$DR \times DD \text{ equals } \tfrac{1}{2} DR, \tfrac{1}{2} DD$$
$$DR \times DR \text{ equals } \tfrac{1}{4} DD, \tfrac{1}{2} DR, \tfrac{1}{4} RR$$
$$DR \times RR \text{ equals } \tfrac{1}{2} DR, \tfrac{1}{2} RR$$

Again taking the average litter as four, this dog will get three DD puppies, six DR puppies and three RR puppies—that is to say, by using a pure dominant sire there would, in twelve puppies, be twice the number of good ones and no really bad ones.

As I wrote earlier, all cases are not so easily worked out as this appears to be, but it must be remembered that, according to so high an authority as Sir Archdall Reid, "The term prepotent, as applied to a parent, implies that his or her character predominates in the blend in any degree up to an inclusive inheritance. To the Mendelian prepotence implies dominance." There is no doubt in my mind that amongst dogs, as amongst horses, there are prepotent sires of a prepotence (though denied by Mendelists) almost amounting to an inclusive inheritance.

Now Galton's Law, as I have explained, means that every ancestor contributes a fraction to the sum total which is the offspring. If an ancestor appears twice in the pedigree then his contribution must of necessity be doubled and if he appears three times his contribution must be

LUSORY

trebled. "Stonehenge"—writing, I believe, before Galton's Law was known of—expresses this very well under another form. He writes, under *The Explanation of a " Hit "* :

"Suppose, for instance, a bitch to be composed of the blood of four different strains, which we will call A, B, C and D : then, if put to a dog composed also of blood from four different strains, one of which was B itself, or a strain like B, but united with others E, F and G, then the produce would be more likely to inherit the characteristics of the B strain than of either A, C, D, E, F or G. If these characteristics are desirable, the result is called a 'hit'; and it is very extraordinary how far back these 'hits' will sometimes go ; the dog and bitch may not be related for six or seven generations, at which point in their pedigrees they may each own a particular dog as their progenitor, and yet their produce will appear to go back to that particular dog in preference to all the others."

Every breeder knows the " hits "—or, as we call them, " nicks "—that occur in the pedigrees of some of the best dogs. The " nick " to Formula in the pedigree of Woodcut is a good example, and Lusory himself shows one to the Herschel—Fair Future combination which threw Faber Fortunæ and Fabulous Fortune. In the extended pedigrees which will be found at the end of the book I have endeavoured to indicate the more prominent "nicks," and readers will probably have no difficulty in finding others.

To apply these theories, if so they can be called : the first point and an essential one is to see that the bitch is free from inborn faults, such as lack of stamina or pluck. A bad-plucked bitch, in my opinion, should at once be discarded from the point of view of a brood bitch—or, for that matter, from any other. Lack of speed and bad working powers must also be taken into account, though I think the former, if combined with plenty of pluck and good working capabilities, can be to a certain extent overlooked. Not only must the bitch be, of herself, free, but her pedigree must also be free from taint. There are several dogs about, the names of which in a pedigree would at once induce me to discard a bitch for breeding purposes. The least sign of " turning it up," however fast either dog or bitch was, should be sufficient and there should be no thought of a second chance or any hope of breeding it out. Bad pluck is bad at any time, but once in a pedigree it is almost impossible, except by close in-breeding to the opposite half of the pedigree, to get it out.

With a bitch with a pedigree that is fair but in which there is, so to speak, nothing to catch hold of, the best result would be obtained by putting her to a dog which is dominant and

Breeding

throwing first-class puppies from all sorts of bitches. There are hundreds of bitches of this type which are the result of outbreeding for generations. Each quartering may contain a Waterloo winner, but each bred in an entirely different way and none of them sufficiently " nicked " to breed in to. The bitches, in themselves, may be really first-class, but they lack backing in their pedigrees—which are, in reality, a mere collection of names.

Then there is the other type of bitch with a Herschel—Thetis, a Herschel—Thoughtless Beauty, a Mellor Moor—Tiny Polly, a Gallant —Gladiole or a Wartnaby—Garbitas combination staring from their pedigrees : these are the bitches to breed from and return the combination blood to from their sires.

Another point not often noted is the fact that a bitch ex a good dam is as a rule a good dam herself. The good-dam qualities are one of the most strongly inherited assets dogs of all breeds possess, and the reverse—the bad-dam qualities —are often equally noticeable. Take the pedigree of Derringer as an example and note how the good-dam qualities run back : Garbitas, Gladiole ; Higher Walton, Formula, Forest Fairy ; Filagree, Flutter of Lace ; Dilwyn, Denwa, Gleneva, Gladiole : or again, Camorra, Thessaly to Thetis in Harmonicon's pedigree.

Before closing this chapter there are three

other points which must be considered, and these are :

(1) Maternal Impressions
(2) Telegony
(3) Saturation

The belief in the first of these dates back to the time of Jacob, who, we are told, placed peeled wands in front of his sheep in order to increase the number of speckled lambs. There are still breeders who follow the example of Jacob, and Professor Wallace in his book, *Farm Live Stock of Great Britain*, writes : " The colour of any object at which an animal looks whilst conceiving or during the early stages of pregnancy may sometimes govern the colour of the young." In support of this view it is mentioned that a breeder " succeeded in preventing his black-polled Angus cows from breeding red or broken calves by putting up a high black fence round the paddock in which he mated them as they came in season, thus preventing them seeing their parti-coloured neighbours." Reference is also made to " one of the most remarkable cases of the influence of imagination on the colour of cattle." In this case Aberdeen Angus cows which never saw cattle of " broken colours " had pure black calves, while cows pastured in a field from which Ayrshire cattle were visible produced several badly marked calves annually. Cossar

Ewart, from whose book the above examples are quoted, explains this as follows :—

" The Angus polled breed is a blend of several varieties which are varied in colour from black through brown, red, and yellow-dun to white. Evidence of this we have from a Banffshire writer who tells us that early in the nineteenth century, though the favourite colour of Aberdeen-Angus cattle was black, the brindles were esteemed, the dun not disliked, but the white or streaked were little sought after. Until it is proved that the broken colours which now and again appear in the polled Angus breed are not due to reversion, it seems unnecessary to believe that they are due to maternal impressions."

This is a fairly typical example of the cases which have been cited in favour of the effect of maternal impressions, and though negative evidence is never entirely satisfactory, there is not sufficient—if there is, indeed, any—positive evidence in support of these impressions to overbalance the negative evidence ; and so long as there are other factors which can feasibly explain these " supposed " cases, there is no necessity to call in the help of " impressions " which, after all, are rather in the same category as dreams. The mother is supposed to receive a mental impression and to transmit it to her offspring as a physical deformity, which, if the explanations of the germinal and somatic cells have been understood, is obviously an impossibility.

The next two headings, Telegony and Saturation, are often considered as synonymous, but, in my opinion, are two different things and should be considered as such.

Telegony can be defined as being the supposed influence of a previous sire on offspring subsequently borne by the same female to a different sire. If, for instance, a pure-bred bitch is accidentally mated with a mongrel dog, or indeed a dog of another breed, it is said by believers in telegony that she is spoilt for future matings as there is a chance of this extraneous blood showing itself in her future offspring. Ewart's experiments with zebras have conclusively negatived this theory and it can nowadays be regarded as nothing more than an old-time myth. The mother is supposed to receive a physical impression and the offspring is said to develop a physical character, but not the character the mother acquired. A negress who has borne a child to a white man and who subsequently bears an exceptionally fair child to a negro has not herself become fair. Her acquirement was, if anything, an impression, and she is supposed to transmit it as a character. Again the categories are different and the theory impossible.

Now to my mind Saturation differs from this in being *not* the influence of a single sire *but* the accumulated influence of several services, and pregnancies, by the same sire. I do not for one moment maintain that supposing a pure-bred bitch were, for instance, mated with and bore puppies to a mongrel dog on, say, three occasions, and then was mated with and bred puppies to a sire of her own race, the first sire to whom she had had three litters would have any influence on the fourth ; but I mean that if the one sire, whether mongrel or pure bred, is used perpetually to the same bitch, each succeeding litter will deteriorate in strength and hardiness in exactly the same way as if there had been a too intensive inbreed.

Bruce Lowe wrote : " With each mating and bearing the dam absorbs some of the nature or actual circulation of the yet unborn foal until she eventually becomes saturated with the sire's nature or blood, as the case may be." During the whole period of gestation the fœtus, of whatever breed, absorbs its nutriment from its mother by way of the fœtal circulation and in the same way excretes its waste products. It is known that constant small doses of drugs or repeated attacks of disease confer an immunity, or call it an increased resistance, to that drug or disease. This means that the tissues are not called upon to respond so actively to that drug or disease. They, so to speak, become accustomed to it. Now it is possible, in fact I think probable, that the tissues of the mother become so accustomed to the products, the fœti, of the one sire that the stimulus becomes insufficient, and less and less nourishment is formed, which reacts on the succeeding litters, or foals, under the guise of weakness.

In no branch of science have two terms been so hopelessly misconstrued and mixed up as those two widely different ones, Telegony and Saturation in the science of Heredity.

V

The Stud Dog and the Brood Bitch

I HAD intended dealing with these two—the Stud Dog and the Brood Bitch—in two entirely separate chapters, but on second thoughts decided that it would be better for some reasons to treat them, or of them, under one heading, and then, when facts and statistics common to both had been considered, to sub-divide and treat of each separately.

One, the most important factor in common, is

THE BEST AGE OF SIRE AND DAM

Looking up old *Stud Books* together with such works of reference as Stonehenge, Goodlake, etc., it is interesting to note what extraordinary variations there are in the ages of sires and dams of famous dogs and bitches. Misterton sired a number of winners at the age of ten and Restorer did the same, whilst Memento was only a puppy when he sired Mineral Water.

In the case of Brood Bitches the variations are even more extraordinary. Czarina, Lord Orford's famous bitch, is said to have been thirteen years of age when she bred Claret and Vengeance ; but of the authentic cases, Raven was eleven years old when she whelped to Herschel, Stitch was eleven when she bred Solo, and Denwa was the same age when she whelped last year to Husky Whisper II. and produced Dilwyn, a Waterloo winner, so far back as 1911. At the other end of the scale, Gay Queen was only fifteen months old when she bred Miss Lively, and Miss Lively divided a stake at which one of her produce did the same thing. Castle Lass was but seventeen months old when she bred Farrenpiece, who divided a thirty-four-dog stake when she was but twelve months old.

These examples are interesting but are rather apart from the heading. To get statistics upon which to base an opinion as to the best age for breeding, I have taken the list of Waterloo Cup winners from its commencement up to the present time, and have tabulated them with the ages of their sires and dams at the time of their birth.

If Table I. is summarised it will be seen that the ages work out as in Tables II. and III. For the sake of completeness, and comparison, I have added " Stonehenge's " summary concerning the ages of greyhounds as collected by him.

Year	Winner	Year Whelped	Sire	Age when Offspring Whelped	Dam	Age when Offspring Whelped
1836	Milanie	?	Milo	?	Nettle or Duchess	?
1837	Fly	?	Tommy Roads	?	Fly	?
1838	Bugle	1835	Bachelor	7?	Nimble	?
1839	Empress	?	Tramp	?	Nettle	?
1840	Earwig	1835	Hailstone	2	Pasterne	2?
1841	Bloomsbury	?	Redcap	?	By Walton, sis. to Preserve	?
1842	Priam	1838	Emperor	3	Venus	3
1843	Major	1841	Moses	4	Melon	4
1844	Speculation	1842	Sandy	4	Enchantress	4
1845	Titania	1842	Driver	7	Zoe	3?
1846	Harlequin	1842	Emperor	7	Lady	?
1847	Senate	1844	Sadek	5	Sanctity	5
1848	Shade	1846	Nonchalance	4	Margery	6
1849	Magician	1846	King Cob	8	Magic	5
1850 1852 1853	Cerito	1848	Lingo	3	Wanton	7
1851	Hughie Graham	1849	Liddesdale	4	Queen of the May	5
1854	Sackcloth	1852	Senate	8	Cinderella	5
1855	Judge	1852	John Bull	4	Fudge	6
1856	Protest	1854	Weapon	3	Pearl	4
1857	King Lear	1854	Wigan	6	Repentance	6
1858	Neville	1856	Autocrat	4	Catherine Hayes	7
1859	Clive	1857	Judge	5	Moeris	5
1856	Selby	1856	Barrator	2	Ladylike	3
1860	Maid of the Mill	1857	Judge	5	Bartolozzi	5
1861	Canaradzo	1858	Beacon	5	Scotland Yet	6

TABLE I—*continued*

Year	Winner	Year Whelped	Sire	Age when Offspring Whelped	Dam	Age when Offspring Whelped
1862	Roaring Meg	1860	Beacon	7	Polly	3
1863	Chloe	1860	Judge	8	Clara	7
1864	King Death	1862	Canaradzo	4	Annoyance	5
1865	Meg	1862	Terrona	4	Fanny Fickle	6
1866	Brigadier	1863	Boreas	8	Wee Nell	3
1867	Lobelia	1865	Sea Foam	5	Lilac	2
1868 1869 1871	Master M'Grath	1866	Dervock	7	Lady Sarah	3
1870	Sea Cove	1868	Strange Idea	3	Curiosity	6
1872	Bed of Stone	1868	Portland	7	Imperatrice	7
1873	Muriel	1871	Fusilier	6	Portia	5
1874	Maguano	1870	Cauld Kail	7	Isoline	3
1875	Honeymoon	1872	Brigadier	9	Hebe	5
1876	Donald	1872	Master Burleigh	9	Phoenix	11
1877 1878	Coomassie	1875	Celebrated	?	Queen	?
1879	Misterton	1877	Contango	7	Lina	6
1880	Honeywood	1876	Cavalier	9	Humming Bird	2
1881	Princess Dagmar	1879	Ptarmigan	4	Gallant Foe	6
1882	Snowflight	1880	Bothal Park	4	Curiosity	6
1883	Wild Mint	1880	Haddo	7	Orla	5
1884	Mineral Water	1881	Memento	1	Erzeroum	5
1885	Bit of Fashion	1883	Paris	4	Pretty Nell	7
1885	Miss Glendyne	1883	Paris	4	Lady Glendyne	7
1886	Miss Glendyne	1883	Paris	4	Lady Glendyne	7

Date	Troughend / Fullerton	Date	Greentick	No.	Toledo / Bit of Fashion	No.
1889	Troughend	1887	Greentick	5	Toledo	6
1889	Fullerton	1887	Greentick	5	Bit of Fashion	4
1890						
1891						
1892						
1893	Character	1890	R. Halliday	7	Mermaiden	8
1894	Texture	1890	Herschel	5	Tinsel	5
1895	Thoughtless Beauty	1892	Herschel	7	Thetis	5
1896	Fabulous Fortune	1894	Herschel	9	Fair Future	7
1897	Gallant	1893	Young Fullerton	4	Sally Milburn	5
1898	Wild Night	1895	Freshman	11	Fine Night	9
1899	Black Fury	1896	Mad Fury	7	Mischief X.	3
1900 / 1901	Fearless Footsteps	1897	Fabulous Fortune	4	Fille de Feu	8
1902	Farndon Ferry	1899	Fiery Furnace	4	Fair Florence	5
1903	Father Flint	1900	Fiery Furnace	5	Fanny Faithful	7
1904	Homfray	1902	Fabulous Fortune	9	Kilmode	9
1905	Pistol II.	1901	Fighting Fire	5	Thessaly	5
1906	Hoprend	1903	Forgotten Fashion	5	Heirloom	4
1907	Long Span	1905	Pateley Bridge	7	Forest Fairy	6
1908	Hallow Eve	1905	Pateley Bridge	7	Forest Fairy	6
1909	Dendraspis	1905	Wartnaby	5	Gleneva	3
1910	Heavy Weapon	1906	Wartnaby	6	Garbitas	7
1911	Jabberwock	1909	Bachelor's Acre	4	Forrester's Favour	10
1912	Tide Time	1910	Friendly Foe.	5	Fast Waves	5
1913	Hung Well	1910	Mandini	7	Pocahontas	5
1914	Dilwyn	1911	Bachelor's Acre	6	Denwa	3
1915	Winning Number	1911	Lottery.	7	Shady	4
1916	Harmonicon	1913	Heavy Weapon	8	Camorra	10
1920	Fighting Force	1917	Forward Foe.	5	Flimsy Finery	4

TABLE II
AGE OF SIRE

	As per Table I.	"Stonehenge's" Statistics
Number got by Sires at 1 year .	1	1
„ „ 2 years .	2	12
„ „ 3 „ .	5	8
„ „ 4 „ .	17	30
„ „ 5 „ .	14	17
„ „ 6 „ .	4	20
„ „ 7 „ .	15	7
„ „ 8 „ .	5	9
„ „ 9 „ .	5	6
„ „ 10 „ .	...	...
„ „ 11 „ .	1	3
	69	113

TABLE III
AGE OF DAM

	As per Table I.	"Stonehenge's" Statistics
Number got by Dams at 1 year .	...	...
„ „ 2 years .	2	7
„ „ 3 „ .	8	25
„ „ 4 „ .	7	20
„ „ 5 „ .	17	21
„ „ 6 „ .	12	12
„ „ 7 „ .	10	9
„ „ 8 „ .	3	3
„ „ 9 „ .	2	...
„ „ 10 „ .	2	1
„ „ 11 „ .	1	...
	64	98

Stud Dog and Brood Bitch

From these tables it can at once be seen that the most successful age for the Stud Dog is four years, as if both series—though in one or two instances they overlap—are taken there are 47 of this age, the next best being at five years with 31. In the case of the Brood Bitch it is somewhat difficult to explain how it is that in my table the best three years are those of five, six and seven, whilst in " Stonehenge's " the best are those of three, four and five, but presumably the greyhound came to maturity earlier—possibly due to sapling racing—then than now, and in my figures, taken over a wider period than he dealt with, they are more evenly balanced. In my table the best age is that of five years and is represented by 17, which, if added to "Stonehenge's" 21, gives 38—a good deal better than any other year.

Another point of interest is that in the case of the most brilliant dogs their sires and dams were of nearly similar age, whilst where there was a considerable difference—an old dog to a young bitch, or vice versa—the produce was not so good.

The next point is

THE BEST MONTH TO BREED

As greyhounds take their ages from the 1st of January in each year it is obvious that one born in mid-January has a certain advantage over one not born until mid-July, but this advantage is, I think, more apparent than real, as the English climate with its extraordinary variations has of necessity to be taken into account. To obtain, so far as is possible, reliable statistics on this matter, I have taken the winning sires, in England, for the season 1919–1920 and tabulated their winning puppy produce according to the months in which they were born, adding in a second column the numbers of litters actually produced by those same sires above and beyond those containing winners. In each case I have added, besides the number of litters, the actual number of puppies named in the *G.S.B.* No account has been taken of any dogs other than puppies whelped in 1918.

TABLE IV

Month Whelped	Winning Litters	Total Litters in 1918 by same Dogs	Winning Puppies	Total Puppies registered in *G.S.B.* vol. by same Dogs	Percentage of Winning Puppies
January . .	4	6	8	21	38·1
February .	8	10	13	33	39·4
March . .	6	11	12	39	30·7
April . .	8	11	14	51	27·4
May . .	11	16	20	82	24·4
June . .	10	12	18	46	39·1
July . .	4	9	6	37	16·2
August . .	1	3	1	9	11·1
September .	...	1	...	8	...
October . .	...	...	...	...	...
November .	1	1	2	4	...
	53	80	94	330	28·4

Stud Dog and Brood Bitch

This table and the percentages given may, at first sight, appear too complicated for explanation, but it can be seen that the two best months are obviously February — or better, January-February — and June. Now all greyhound puppies are taken care of at birth, as people do not breed them, pay big stud fees and go through all the necessary trouble if they do not intend to look after the bitch and puppies at the time of whelping. For this reason I think the actual month of whelping is unimportant, but the important time is *the time of weaning*. Puppies born in January and February are ready for weaning about mid-April or early May, which, in this country, are usually fine months, and June puppies are ready for weaning towards the end of August, when the weather usually clears for September. April and May puppies run the risk of the heat—when there is any—of July and early August, whilst the July and August puppies get the cold of October and November before they are really old enough to stand it. The whole point is that at weaning time the puppies cannot stand excessive heat or cold and that those do best that are weaned in the spring or autumn.

From the generalised points I must now turn to the detail of

The Stud Dog

At the present time breeders have the choice

of some thirty or forty stud dogs which are advertised from time to time in the Sporting Press. At least two-thirds of these are never likely, by any stretch of the imagination, to sire a winner, and it becomes a matter of importance for the novice breeder to be able to delete these and then make a choice from the remaining third. In the first place, when picking a sire for a greyhound bitch, there must be no thought whatsoever as to the amount of the stud fee or the distance it is necessary to travel to take the bitch there. A greyhound bitch that is worth breeding from is worth putting to the dog most likely to suit her blood, irrespective of cost, and, what is more, she is worth taking to him personally. No one ever takes as much trouble over an owner's property, or dog, as he does himself.

Now the process of selection : First it is necessary to go thoroughly into the dog's pedigree and see that there is plenty of running blood in it, especially on the dam's side, and also a name, or combination of names, which will nick with the same name or combination in the dam's pedigree. The nick should not be too close up, but, say, with two or three generations free on either side, and if possible it should be strengthened by a more remote nick which will act as a backing up.

The next point is the elimination of all dogs with any sign of weakness. A dog that has

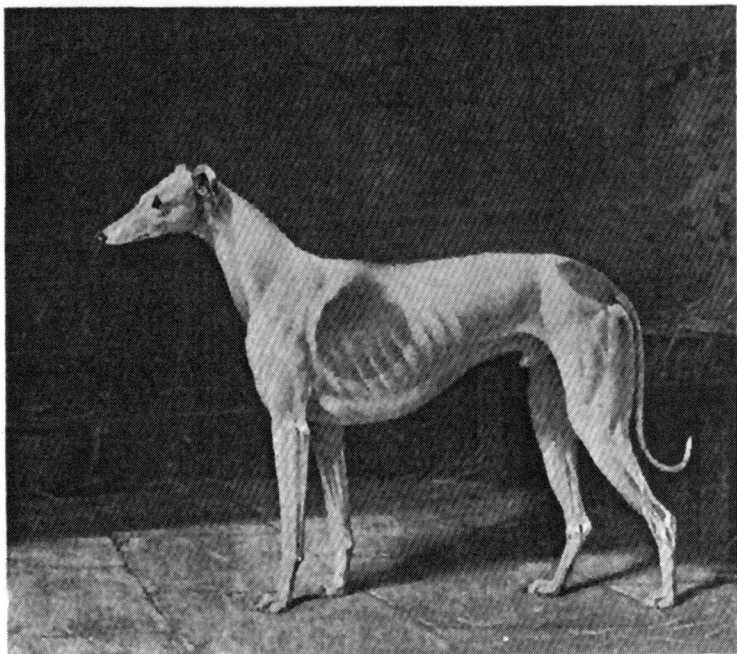

KING COB

After the painting by Barraud. By kind permission of Mr. John Looker

once "turned it up" should never be used, and the pedigree must be closely examined for any dog appearing in it close up that has evidenced this failing. Colour I do not think is important, though personally I am very much averse to "blues"—I know that MacPherson, Gloomy, etc., were "blues"—as I think that for some reason, maybe 'tis imagination, they and their produce do not run as straight, or put as much in, as the others.

Next the *Stud Books* should be examined to see what sort of produce the dog has been siring and out of what sort of bitches, and, if it is in any way possible, a visit should be made to one of the various meetings to see some of the produce run, or the sporting papers—*The Sportsman, The Sporting Chronicle* and *The Sporting Life* all give detailed reports—should be watched to see how the puppies run their courses. Some dogs seem to sire fast but wild puppies who are in reality overfast and run "all wings" at the turns. Others sire puppies that are slower but who work their game, when they get in, better and who never give a chance away, and these latter are, in big stakes, the more satisfactory type to own.

One last point, and I think an important one, is that it is wiser not to use a Stud Dog for at least twelve months after he has been out of training. Training and the rigour of the diet are not good for breeding purposes and it is much better to allow a good rest between the two before using him. Some breeders, I know, rush at a dog as soon as possible after he has made his name, and some, even, use him before he has finished coursing, but, all the same, I am certain I am right, and there are always plenty of good dogs of good standing to use without having resource to new and untried ones.

Someone, possibly more than one, will criticise this chapter and say, or write, that I have said nothing about shape or make. . . . They run and win in all shapes and of all makes, and so long as a greyhound can gallop and work it does not matter what he looks like. This work is not written for the owners of those apologies, "The Exhibition Greyhound," but for the coursing man, and he, I know, will understand my point.

The Brood Bitch

Now comes the question of the Brood Bitch, and the big question at the start is as to whether it is better to breed from a big-stake winner or not. Big-stake winners such as Bab-at-the-Bowster, Rebe, Tollwife, Bed of Stone and Scotland Yet have been good brood bitches, but there are hundreds of others as good, if not better, that never won or divided a stake in their lives. Coursing and training have a distinct effect on the sexual functions, as is evidenced by the frequent irregularity of the bitches' "seasons." I have, personally, had bitches that have come in season three times in the year, and, on the other hand, have had some that have only been on once in the year and that in midsummer. It stands to reason that the running, the excitement, the rigours of training and the hard galloping must have some effect, and though I would not go so far as to say that I would not breed from a big-stake winner, I think it infinitely preferable, if possible, to breed from her litter sister who has not been so hard run. Again I think it is advisable to allow a rest between coursing and breeding and should certainly not use a bitch for at least six or eight months after she has been "turned out" of training.

In advising a novice, a one-dog man, on starting a kennel, I have always recommended the purchase of a bitch as a beginning, and one of my reasons for advocating the purchase of a first, or second, season bitch is that the owner knows exactly the amount of running and training the bitch has had or has. The candle cannot be burnt at both ends and if the bitch was bought as a brood bitch then the less actual coursing she has the better for her brood prospects.

Another point is that a brood bitch at every stage of her life must be treated with care at the time of her seasons. The generative system is by

far the most delicate and highly organised of all,
and bitches in season should be treated for the time
being almost as invalids, and fed and exercised
accordingly. If this were done throughout their
puppyhood there would be far more regularity
in their seasons later on in life. Again, a very
great deal of harm is often done by coursing
bitches too soon after their seasons. After a
bitch has been in season she puts on fat internally
and ought never to be raced, or even trained,
until at least ten weeks after all signs of œstrum,
or heat, have passed.

These points can only be watched and attended
to if the bitch is bought in her early days and
therefore I again advise, without apologising for
repetition, the purchase of the future brood bitch
early.

Now her pedigree must be good, and one
point that must be insisted on is that she is herself out of a good dam. It is extraordinary how
a good brood bitch goes back through her dam
and grand-dam, etc., through a perfect line of
good dams. There is no stronger inherited trait
than the good, or bad, dam qualities and it is
one of the first things to make certain of in
purchasing a bitch. A good brood bitch is a
treasure ; a bad one a perpetual nuisance and
disappointment.

Next, the point of size must be considered,
and I think the small, neat bitch makes, as a

rule, the better mother. She is quicker on her feet, not so clumsy as her bigger sisters, and if a bit small for coursing, is none the worse for it. The big, roomy bitch that would be picked in any other breed is not so generally satisfactory, and I most distinctly recommend the small one.

This, I think, covers the more important points of both Stud Dog and Brood Bitch, without, I hope, overlapping other chapters. Both are difficult subjects for didactic treatment, as so much more can be learnt from actual experience in these matters than from a book.

VI

The Management of the Brood Bitch

Œstrum or Season

BITCHES as a rule come in season twice a year, but, probably due to training, etc., greyhounds are very irregular and many only come on once in the twelve months; whilst some may even miss a complete year. Bessy Bedlam, dam of Bedlamite, was never in season until the age of five years.

This lack of regularity forms almost a disease, like the dysmenorrhœa of the human being, and, even after training is over, never seems to right itself. Once a bitch is irregular in her seasons, she always will be, and it is a mistake to conclude that because a bitch comes in season in May she will repeat it in November and so be just right for January puppies. A great deal of irregularity is due to the lack of attention paid by owners and trainers to bitches at the time of season. In the first place, at the first sign of its onset, evidenced by a colourless discharge and a slight swelling of the parts, all meat should at once be omitted from the diet, which should be changed to that which would be used for an invalid.

The Brood Bitch

Fish, rice puddings, sloppy food, etc., are all good, and a mild laxative, such as an eight-grain rhubarb pill, is an additional help. All heating foods must be assiduously avoided.

Again, all heavy exercise must be stopped, both for the duration of the " heat " and for at least two months afterwards. It is annoying, one knows, to see a bitch come in season in September and to know that she should not be raced until after Christmas, but there it is, and if bitches are kept they must be treated properly or will be utterly spoilt. Slow walking exercise is ample, or, better still, if there is an enclosed yard the bitch may be left to exercise herself. No attempt should be made at galloping until at least ten weeks after the cessation of all signs of heat.

If it is intended to breed from the bitch, she should be isolated, and as soon as possible after the coloured discharge—which follows upon the colourless after a period of about a week—has stopped she should be put to the dog.

In many books detailed particulars of the different stages of heat are given. Normally, the colourless discharge should last a week and then be followed by a blood-stained discharge which should also last about a week and which, in turn, should be followed by a colourless, glairy discharge lasting from two days up to a week. The parts are swollen all through but most markedly so during the second stage. These details must be remembered, but at the same time, like the "seasons," the variations from them, at any rate in the greyhound, are far more common. Bitches may be on and off season in under a week, whilst others may go almost a full month. Some may be obviously in season ; others would be missed if they were not examined. The chief point is the blood-stained discharge, and the right time for service is as early as possible after it has stopped.

Arrangements should be made with the owner of the stud dog some time before the bitch is due on season, as it is impossible, with probably the coursing season in full swing, to arrange times and places at a minute's notice when she is actually in season. As soon as the "colour" stops she should be taken to the stud dog. I have written "taken," as I think it is a great mistake to send bitches about the country, especially when in season, in boxes unaccompanied. They are upset, nervous, excited, etc., just when it is all the better for them to be quiet. If a brood bitch is worth breeding from, she is worth the trouble of taking to the stud dog personally. Besides the advisability of doing this from the point of view of the bitch, it is also advisable to see the stud dog. It is not common, one knows, but at the same time it is possible for the stud dog that has been selected to be " off colour " or

The Brood Bitch

ill and his services to be replaced by those of another who, though possibly equally good, is not so well known nor as fashionable. Rather than disappoint the owner of the bitch, the owner, or trainer, of the stud dog replaces him by another, with the result that the owner of the bitch pays a high price for the services of the fashionable dog but instead of getting a litter of puppies by him gets them by an inferior, or not so fashionable, one. The result is that the puppies' pedigrees are incorrect and it is impossible to ever mate them with any hope of breeding a winner except by accident. This practice was, I believe, at one time a common one, but nowadays is rare ; nevertheless, it must be borne in mind, and the owner who is able to pay a fifteen-guinea stud fee must not stop at the pound or two that it will cost him to take the bitch to the dog himself.

Neither dog nor bitch should be fed for twelve hours before the service. After the service the bitch should be fed and allowed to rest quietly for an hour or two before being removed. If the distance from the stud dog necessitates a train journey, it is better for the bitch to be allowed to remain quiet overnight, after the service, and taken home the next day.

There is, I know, a difference of opinion as to the desirability or otherwise of a double service, but I think that one service, at the right time, is quite sufficient and it is only upsetting the bitch to repeat it.

Pregnancy : The duration of pregnancy varies round a mean of sixty-three days, sometimes being two days under and as often two days over. I have had a bitch go a full week over time, have a normal parturition and a normal litter, but this is an exceptional case and need only be noted.

During the first three weeks the bitch should be rested and fed on invalid diet, and at the end of that time should be treated for worms, preferably by Sherley's capsules. There is, I am certain, a very great deal in this treatment of the brood bitch for worms, and the details given in another chapter should be followed.

After this, for the next two weeks the exercise may be given more freely and even short gallops or a romp after a tennis ball may be allowed, but after five weeks it is risky to do anything much beyond exercise on the lead. The feeding after the first three weeks should be liberal and nutritious : horse meat, cow-heels, etc., may be given freely, but the carbohydrate, or cereal part of the feeding, must not be overdone. The object must be to give as nutritious feeds as possible in as small a compass as will satisfy and the stomach must on no account be overladen.

During the last three weeks the meat in the feeds must be increased in order to ensure an abundant supply of milk. Milk is rich in protein and can only be formed from protein-containing food, of which the best, and most natural for the dog, is meat, and, in consequence, this must not be stinted. It is best given cooked, and the resulting soup poured over whatever is used to thicken it—brown bread, Melox, porridge, etc. —but it should not be fed too thick : sloppy feeds in the last stages are essential.

It is just these details that make all the difference between good and bad results. One often hears of bitches being short of milk, etc., but when investigated it can be seen, in nine cases out of ten, that the trouble is not the fault of the bitch, but is due to wrong feeding on the part of the owner. Milk cannot be made out of air, and proteins cannot be made from carbohydrates.

Three days before the bitch is due to whelp she should be given a dose of

℞ Castor Oil   .   .   .   . $\frac{1}{2}$ oz.
   Syrup of Buckthorn .   .   . $\frac{1}{2}$ oz.

on an empty stomach. This clears her well out without causing straining.

Parturition : The next point is the housing of the bitch during parturition. All through the book I have written, as far as possible, from the point of view of the small owner, and in this case need make no exception. The ideal brood bitch kennel, or maternity hospital, must be heated, and the ideal method is, in my opinion, by means of hot-water pipes running under the bench on the same system as the heating of a greenhouse. There is no necessity, in fact it is objectionable, to pamper a bitch, but when puppies are expected in the Januarys, Februarys and Marches of our climate, and a big stud fee has been paid, it is necessary to take some precautions. The best place for whelping is a large, roomy loose-box with a bench raised eighteen inches to two feet above the floor, and a two-inch hot-water pipe running right round the box and underneath the bench, connecting up with a stove outside. The bench should have a ledge all round at least six inches high and sloping inwards so that the bitch does not lie against the bottom of it but leaves a space behind her into which a puppy can crawl and so obviate being laid upon.

The best litter is undoubtedly straw, cut up into short lengths and distributed freely on the bench. Hay is objectionable as, though warmer, it is apt to steam when it gets warm and then acts as a kind of vapour bath which is injurious to the puppies.

Towards the time of pupping the bitch becomes restless, goes off her food, and there is swelling and discharge from the vagina. Directly this appears she should have a well-warmed old rug put on and be left alone. Greyhound bitches very seldom have any trouble in pupping, and are much better left alone and not upset by constant intrusions.

Directly it is all over, or apparently the last puppy has been born, the bitch should be given a good feed of Benger's Food with a tablespoonful of brandy in it. Then her hind legs should be dried down, the vagina washed with a weak solution of Lysol and water (a teaspoonful to a pint of water is strong enough), the bedding changed, the old rug replaced by a clean *warm* one, and, after seeing that the puppies are sucking properly, she may be left to sleep comfortably. I do not believe in pulling the bitch about to see if there are more puppies present, as if she has had, say, five or six, and an hour or more has elapsed since the last was born, the probabilities are that there is only one more, if any, to come, and it will not make much difference to the general cleanliness—and, at any rate, the bitch will be more comfortable.

For the first three days after whelping, the bitch should have nothing but sloppy food : Benger's Food, fish, milk puddings, etc. After this she should be gradually got on to solid food, until, if all goes well, she may on the fifth day have a meat and meal feed. After the second day she should be encouraged to leave the box night and morning to relieve herself, and from the end of the first week onwards should be kept out a little longer each time, until at the end of the third week she is out for about half-an-hour night and morning. Exercise need not be bothered with, but she must be walked about, on a lead, and care must be taken that she does not get cold. A brisk run will do her good.

Directly the puppies' eyes are open—usually about the tenth day—they should be encouraged to lap, and the best food for them, though they will waste most of it at first, is either " Glaxo " or

Cow's Milk . . . . 7 oz.
Plasmon . . . . 1 tablespoonful
Cream (Ideal Milk) . . 1 tablespoonful
Water.
Mix the Plasmon into a paste with the water; add the milk; well mix, and boil. When cool, add the cream, and feed.

This should be given after the bitch has been away for a while and immediately before she returns. For the first day or two too much success must not be looked for, but gradually the whelps get into the way of lapping and it becomes easy. If the whelps are fed regularly in this way night and morning from the third week on, and the litter is not a big one, there is no hurry to start weaning before the end of the sixth week. At the end of the fourth week the Plasmon mixture or the Glaxo should be thickened with a little very fine well-boiled oatmeal, to which, if the puppies are at all purged, a little arrowroot has been added, and at the end of the fifth week they should have mutton broth, made by boiling sheeps' heads, with a little of the meat finely minced added to it and the broth thickened with either oatmeal or Robinson's Barley.

During the whole of the time she is suckling the bitch must be well fed, and besides an unlimited supply of meat she should have at least a quart of milk during the day, either alone or made up with Benger's Food.

Weaning : At the end of the sixth week weaning should be commenced. This must be done gradually, so that, as far as possible, the puppies go from their mother to other food without a break. At first she should be taken away in the morning and not put back to them until late at night, just after they have been fed. The whelps must be fed at regular intervals, say at six o'clock in the morning, eleven o'clock, four o'clock and at nine o'clock, and the bitch should not be returned to them until after this last feed. After three or four days of this routine, she should be taken away all day, put back with them for a couple of hours at night, taken away all night and put back for an hour in the morning. Then after another three or four days the morning visit can be stopped and two days later she can be taken away altogether.

Once this has been done she should be given

a good dose of salts—a tablespoonful of milk—to clear her out and help to stop the secretion of milk. Then her breasts should be well rubbed with camphorated oil and her food should be given dry. In nearly every case this is effectual and in two or three days all secretion of milk stops and the bitch dries up.

Now the whelps. Weaning is, perhaps, the most anxious time of all, as if it is not done gradually, and they have not started lapping early enough, they go all to pieces for no apparent rhyme or reason. The first thing to do, when they have left their mother, is to treat them for worms, and this is best done by means of that most effective remedy, " Ruby," the great advantage of which is that, besides removing the worms, it acts as a tonic to the whelps. The treatment must be done thoroughly and according to the directions, as a half-wormed puppy is always a bother and a weakling. Once worming is over, the whelps, weather permitting, should be got out of doors and if possible given full liberty in a wired-in paddock. The feeding is important and the difference between the fat content of the bitch's milk and that of ordinary food must never be forgotten and must be allowed for in some way. Cod-liver oil, Virol or lard should be given in every meal.[1]

---

[1] The Polienta Co. have just put an excellent cod-liver oil and malt biscuit upon the market.

The Brood Bitch

Worms and rickets are the cause of 90 per cent. of the mortality in whelps, and the former must be got rid of and the latter guarded against. The research work that has been done on the causation of rickets has proved it to be due entirely to a deficiency in the accessory food factor, Fat Soluble A.

The effects of damp, draughts, overcrowding, etc., can all be overcome if Fat Soluble A is present in sufficient quantity, and owners, breeders and trainers must remember this and see that in each feed there is a sufficiency of it.

Foster Mothers : I can hardly conclude this chapter without some reference to the necessity of "foster mothers." A greyhound bitch, as a rule, has more puppies than she herself can bring up, and it is a moot point, still open to argument, as to whether the whelps over and above a certain number should be destroyed or whether the services of a foster mother should be obtained.

Both have arguments pro and con, but for the small owner and breeder I think the better way is to destroy the weaklings, well feed the mother and let her do the nursing. For the large breeder, with every convenience, a foster mother has advantages in that every puppy can be reared, and the best way is to arrange some time beforehand, by advertising, for either a bull-terrier or a retriever due to whelp about the same time.

The Greyhound & Coursing

These two breeds are, as a rule, good mothers, and can always be depended upon. In all cases it is best to muzzle the foster mother for at least twenty-four hours and to gradually substitute the greyhound puppies for her own, leaving one or two of her own with her until she gets settled to the new-comers. If as the greyhounds are substituted they are well rubbed over with the urine or manure of the foster mother's puppies, she will take to them more readily.

The change should not be attempted until the greyhound whelps are at least two days old, as there is a substance—colustrum—in the bitch's milk, for the first two days, the action of which is a mild purgative and clears the bowels of the whelps. As soon as they have had this they can be put to the foster mother, who should have whelped as nearly as possible at the same time as the greyhound.

It must never be forgotten that King Death was fostered by a bull-dog bitch.

VII

Saplings and Puppies

WITH the whelps weaned, the novice breeder is apt to pat himself on the back and think that it is simply a matter of time before they make their bow to the public, and only a little longer before Wilkinson slips them for the final in the Waterloo or Smith officiates in a similar way somewhere down south. The whole thing looks easy, but it is not one-hundredth part as easy as it looks, and the novice breeder, with half-a-dozen really nice whelps, has many difficulties to overcome and almost certainly many disappointments before ever any of his whelps reaches the age of saplings, not to mention puppies. Here it is as well to make the terms "saplings" and "puppies" clear:

A sapling is a greyhound whelped on or after the 1st of January of the year in which the season commenced.

A puppy is a greyhound which was whelped after the 1st of January in the year *preceding* the commencement of the season of running.

For example, a greyhound whelped in February

1920 is a whelp until the coursing season 1920–1921 commences, when he becomes a sapling, and remains as such until the commencement of the season 1921–1922, when he becomes a puppy, though actually of the age (taking the commencement of the season to be in October) of one year and eight months.

Once thoroughly weaned, *and* wormed, the question arises as to whether the whelps should be kept at home or sent out to "walks." There are pros and cons on both sides, and the really important point is the space, time and accommodation at the disposal of the breeder. Greyhound whelps must have liberty, and if the breeder is the fortunate possessor of, say, two or three acres of land, has the means to fence it, or part of it, with six-foot kennel railings, or small-mesh wire-netting, and has the time to thoroughly look after his whelps—then, but only then, they are best at home ; otherwise they are better divided up and sent to reliable "walks." With roads almost entirely devoted to motor traffic, such "walks" are becoming more and more difficult to find. In the old days the village butcher made an excellent "walker," as he, as a rule, was fond of dogs and had the very best possible food for them at his very elbow ; but nowadays the village roads are infested with motor chars-à-bancs, motor bicycles, etc., and no dog running loose has much chance of surviving more than, if so much as, a week. Again, the country farmer was in the old days a better friend to the greyhound than he is to-day. Then he liked them, made them "at home" and looked after them ; but nowadays, in many cases, he regards them as poachers and if living in a harrier country will as likely as not have nothing to do with them. Still, I think the owner's hopes of good "walks" lie mostly in this direction, and if he is lucky enough to get on to one of the genuine old-time farmers who take an interest in coursing he will have found a "walk" that many are looking for but few fortunate enough to find.

"Stonehenge" puts the case for home rearing very concisely. He objects to "walks" for the following reasons :—

(1) Few farmers or butchers really take any interest in the greyhound for its own sake ; they only rear them as a favour to the party giving them in charge.

(2) If any disease attacks the puppies, much time is lost before the proper remedy can be applied.

(3) The food is not given regularly, and seldom of sufficiently good quality, and it is not carefully boiled, from which cause tapeworm is so common amongst dogs reared "at walk."

(4) They are liable to all sorts of accidents from kicks, etc.

(5) They lie about in the wet and cold, contracting thereby rheumatism, and also from cold habitually setting up their backs till they grow into that form called "wheel-back."

(6) They are always getting into mischief and receiving severe punishment for so doing, by which their spirit is broken, and they lose that fire which ought to be carefully preserved.

The "favour," by the way, now amounts to at least 5s., more often 10s., per week per head.

To take first the rearing of whelps at home. From the age of weaning until they are five or six months old the whelps are all the better with absolute freedom, and the best way to allow this is to kennel them in a kennel on wheels, much after the style of a movable poultry house, and to place this inside, or make it form one end of, a wire run of, say, twenty to thirty feet in length by twelve to fifteen feet in width. If the run is made of wire-netting threaded on to iron stakes it can be moved with the kennel from place to place, as the land becomes stale and sodden, without much trouble. The netting must be at least six feet high and of fine (half-inch) mesh, as greyhound whelps seem to have a wonderful power of getting over or through anything.

The kennel should be so constructed that it can be closed up entirely in the event of the weather being cold or wet, and be fitted with a bench raised well off the ground and the space between it and the ground boarded up so that the whelps cannot get underneath. On the bench a good thickness of straw should be placed so that there is no fear of the whelps feeling the cold. In this they can cuddle up together and keep each other warm. Hay is advised by some, but it is not a good bedding, as it is very rarely absolutely dry and, directly it becomes warm, is apt to steam and so predispose to rheumatism and colds.

The feeding should be regulated by the fact that bitch's milk contains 14 per cent. of butter-fat, hence an extraordinarily large quantity of the accessory food factor, Fat Soluble A. If the analyses of the milks of different species of animals are compared, it will be seen that the faster the species normally grow, the higher the butter-fat content of their mother's milk. Dogs are exceptionally fast-growing animals; their mothers' butter-fat content is, in consequence, high, and it is necessary when this is stopped to replace it by foods particularly rich in butter-fat. A food with a butter-fat percentage of 3·5 would be quite suitable for the rearing of a calf but would cause rickets in a dog. The butter-fat itself, or the lack of it, does not cause the trouble, but it contains the Fat Soluble A., a deficiency of which is the cause of rickets.

This may seem laboured, but upon it a great deal of the success of rearing depends. If the analysis of the foods, given in another chapter, is referred to, it will be seen that horse meat—particularly the breast—is the richest in both protein and fat, and this should be made the basis of all diets. For whelps, I think the best way is to mince the meat, place it in plenty of water, add salt and allow it to simmer slowly either in a boiler, a Parrish's steam cooker, or a slow oven. When it is thoroughly cooked, the meat should be removed and the liquid brought up to the boil and thickened with either oatmeal, whole flour or brown bread : this is then cooled, the meat replaced and the whole fed as a semi-solid mass. As a further preventive of rickets, raw green vegetables, minced, may be mixed with the food, or cabbage water or, better still, lettuce water may be used. This must be made by putting the vegetables into *cold* water and allowing it to simmer thoroughly before bringing it to the boil. This water may be then added to the meat-soup, or, if preferred, it may be used to simmer the meat in.

Again, as a preventive of rickets—and it is worth preventing—a small dose of cod-liver oil[1] or Virol (a teaspoonful) should be given night and morning.

So long as the motions remain of a yellowish-brown colour the feeding is correct, but any looseness of the bowels (due probably to too much fat), or blackness of the motions (due to too much meat), must be at once counteracted. Looseness is, as a rule, best treated by giving an occasional feed of *well*-boiled rice, whilst the

[1] Codolettes are ideal for this.

136

black stools can be relieved by dropping the meat to a certain extent.

After the age of six months, I think the whelps', or as often as not the saplings', liberties should be to a certain extent curtailed. They must now be got used to the collar and lead, and this must be done with as little upset as possible. At first a collar should be put on in the run and left on until the dog gets used to it ; then a lead should be attached and the dog allowed to become gradually accustomed to it. There must be no attempt at leading or expecting the dog to follow for some time. Everything must be done gradually and the dog allowed to gain full confidence.

When this has been done, they should be removed to their permanent kennels (which should be on the same plan as the movable one) and only allowed out for an hour night and morning. In this way, I think, the dogs come out with more fire, do more in the time and get better stretched than if they are at liberty all the time. This must be combined with a certain amount of road work to get the feet hard and the bones knit up. It must not be too strenuous, nor too long, but of the night and morning hour at least half should be slow work on the roads on the lead. Some writers advise exercise behind a bicycle, but I only mention this to condemn the practice, as it is not the kind of exercise that is suitable for, or applicable to, greyhounds. The feeding during this time should be on the same lines as advised for the earlier months. Dogs should now be separated from the bitches.

This brings the saplings to the end of their sapling season, and they can be turned up and summered, in much the same way as is done with older dogs. I have omitted all mention of sapling trials, as I do not think they are either necessary or beneficial. Saplings are too young to risk at hares, and to course greyhounds at any other game than the hare is to ask for trouble. Rabbits turn far more quickly than a hare, and if saplings are entered to them there will sooner or later be an accident and the best, in all probability, of the litter broken down for good. Many a good greyhound has broken a leg in coursing a rabbit.

During the summer they may be allowed to take it easy until August, when strict training must start for the coming season. This I have gone into fully in another chapter, but there are one or two points that must be mentioned.

The first of these is that the puppy must be taught to kill. A greyhound that is soft-mouthed and " nurses " a hare takes far more out of himself and gets far longer and heavier courses than one that is a hard killer. I have tried many ways of teaching them, but I think the best is to enter them to rats. Once a greyhound, or any other plucked dog, gets nipped by a rat, he never wastes much time over killing the next, and I have noticed that a greyhound good at rats is, as a rule, a hard killer when it comes to a hare. He, or she, keeps that bit of extra "up his [or her] sleeve" that enables them to kill whilst their opponent is thinking about it.

The next point is the "slips." A slip-shy greyhound is useless. The best way to teach them to get well away from slips is to put a pair in and slip them to someone they know and who is armed with a bit of meat, but there must be no bungling with the slipping and the novice had better learn to slip on a pair of old greyhounds, who know the game and will help him, before he tries his hand on puppies and by a bungle spoils them. There is an art in it which can only be learnt by experience.

Lastly, there is the question of trials. Personally I am no great believer in home trials and think that by far the better and more sporting way is to try the puppies in public. Of course, every puppy must be entered to his game before being coursed in public, but the better way to do this is to slip him, if one is sure of one's slipping, with a second or third season dog at a hare somewhere where it is to some extent possible to regulate the length of the course. Small fields and big hedges will help with this, but do not slip a puppy for the first time in a place where there is any chance of him getting a real gruelling. If it is possible, it will add to his education if arrangements are made for one of the well-known slippers to officiate with the slips.

This "entering to game" may be carried out any time after he is fit to run, but I do not believe in really coursing puppies too early in the season. Give them an easy time—an odd course or two, if there is a big stake going, will do them good and if the puppies are bitches the earlier they are run the better, but as far as possible let them off lightly until after Christmas. An overrun puppy rarely does much good later on, and it is farcical to expect one to come out at Lowther and run a stake a month from then on until the Barbican without feeling it. He, or she, may win stakes as a puppy but not after, and there is the additional risk of their being spoilt for the later life duties at the Stud.

A greyhound puppy should never under any circumstance be allowed to know, or realise, his or her limit, but must always be treated in such a way that everything he or she does looks easy and natural. Let them "kid" themselves until it is absolutely necessary for them to go all out. The time for this will come and it will then be time enough.

VIII

Training

IN the training of anything, man, horse or dog, the whole secret depends upon an intimate knowledge of the individuality of the subject under training. What is one dog's meat may be another's poison, and to be successful as a trainer it is absolutely necessary to know and understand each dog's little eccentricities and whims. Some dogs do well on horse-flesh ; others do not. Some do better when kennelled with a companion ; others prefer to be alone. Some are delicate feeders and must be tempted ; others are worse than the proverbial pig and must be restrained. All these and a thousand and one little things must be noticed, remembered and understood ; otherwise the game is better left alone. The man who feeds and trains half-a-dozen greyhounds all on the same food and each the same amount of exercise may occasionally, by good luck, have one fit, but he is not a real trainer.

If these limitations are understood, and remembered, the following hints on training—learnt by experience and not, as is so commonly the case, copied from other books—may be of use.

The Greyhound & Coursing

In the first place, I like to see all greyhounds summered—that is to say, let down and roughed up immediately after their last course of the season. This means more work in training, but the rest they have had through it does them good, and when they come up in August for training proper there is something to work on. A half-trained greyhound in August is useless and, as a rule, more bother than it is worth. It has to be remembered that the trainer—who is maybe the owner also—has probably likewise been roughed up and summered and, like his dog, has also to be got fit. If both dog and trainer are out of condition, so much the better, as both get fit gradually without either overdoing it.

For coursing early in October, mid-August is late enough to start, and the first thing to be done is to get the dogs clean inside and out. A 6 to 8 grain compound rhubarb pill is the best treatment for the former, and for the latter Keating's powder is excellent, especially if the powder is rubbed well in and then the dog rugged up over it. This may seem unnecessary, but fleas and nits are a constant source of irritation and the fitter the dog becomes the more they appear to worry him, and in consequence he is much better rid of them at the start.

Now for the exercise. For the first two weeks, six miles slow walking—by "slow" I mean six miles in two hours—is ample, and then

Harmonicon, Winner Waterloo Cup, 1916

the dogs should be rubbed down when they come in. The walking should be on metal or macadam roads, if it is possible to find any, as this gets the feet hard and the nails short directly, and is far preferable to walking on country roads or lanes with soft surfaces. The feet and nails should be examined as soon as the dogs come into the kennels after exercise, and if there is any sign of soreness the road work must be eased up and the feet bathed with salt and water—a teaspoonful to half-a-pint. Some dogs will go through their whole life with hard feet and unbroken nails, whilst others are a perpetual nuisance. A bitch I have in mind was everlastingly shedding the horny layer of her pads and would be lame for weeks on end through it. The least bit of frost on the ground seemed to start them and, once started, nothing (and I tried most things) had the least effect. During the first fortnight the ordinary food can be continued, and I have found Melox, made with boiling water and allowed to stand, as good an ordinary, every-day feed as anything.

At the end of the fortnight—that is to say, about the first week in September—the real work must begin.

The length of the walk need not be increased, but the time in which the six miles are covered must be considerably reduced, until they can be completed in, as nearly as possible, an hour and a quarter. This, I know, takes some doing, and during the first week of it both dogs and trainer will have had enough, but gradually both commence to get fitter and the exercise becomes a pleasure rather than a trial.

On arrival home each dog must be rubbed down. This is best done by standing over the dog and with a rough massage glove (Spratts make a very good one) on one hand the muscles of the neck are rubbed, always going with the lie of the hair ; then the muscles of the shoulder and then the forelegs. Take time over it and do it thoroughly, the bare hand doing one side and the gloved one the other. Then after, say, five minutes, change the glove over to the other hand and repeat the rubbing. From the forelegs, come along the body to the loins and quarters and do these with a good swing, more easily learnt than described, coming along the loins and down the front muscles of the thighs with the ball of the thumb doing the work. Then, turning round and facing towards the tail, do the hips and buttocks in the same way. A good rubbing will take at least twenty minutes to do properly, but it is worth doing and saves a lot of exercise on the roads. Directly this is finished, the dogs must be rugged up, fed and made comfortable. I do not believe in rugging up too early, but once the massage is begun and the feeding altered, it is absolutely necessary.

Ordinary food contains a great proportion of carbohydrates and fats, and these during digestion are oxidised and in the process give off heat. Directly the strict training diet is started the carbohydrates and fats are of necessity reduced to a minimum and the proteins, or albuminoids, increased to a maximum ; hence the heat produced is less and must be made up for with rugs. For exercising, I think covert-coating is ideal for the rugs, as they are light and yet waterproof, whilst for kennel use kersey cloth of the best quality is necessary. The number of rugs used in the kennel must depend entirely on the individual dog.

The feeding must now be gradually altered and meat included in the dietary. Opinions, I know, differ, but I think it is more digestible if lightly cooked, just so that it is like an underdone beef-steak. Before the war it was difficult to get satisfactory horse-meat, but now, with the Belgian shops everywhere, it is possible to get horse-flesh that is passed as fit for human consumption, and this is cheaper and, on analysis, better than cow-meat. The Melox must be dropped and replaced with brown bread, and this must always be stale. To start, use a little Melox, some stale bread and a quarter of a pound of meat, gradually dropping out the Melox and increasing the bread and meat until the evening meal consists of half a large loaf of stale brown bread with half-a-pound of meat slowly cooked, cut up, and the juice poured over the bread.

It is recommended in many books that oatmeal should be used in the form of porridge. For summering dogs, if given with plenty of vegetables, it is useful, but it is a hopeless food for training, as anyone will understand who tries to catch a train after a heavy breakfast of porridge.

After a week of this feeding, as the main feed, with a biscuit or a slice of stale brown bread as the morning feed, the gallops may be started, but these must not be done too soon after the change of food. Many and many a dog is ruined by being galloped on unsuitable feeding. A horse can be steadied and made to go at a slow gallop or even a canter, but a greyhound, if of any use, is "all out" every time and all the time, and a gallop on fattening food will do more harm than if he never had a gallop. Don't be tempted to hurry ; the walking exercise and the massage are the chief factors in getting the dogs fit—the gallops are only to sharpen them up. Some books will say that the gallops are also to "clear their wind," but if my instructions are carried out I do not think there should ever be the least sign of "thick wind," which in nine cases out of ten is actually caused by galloping on unsuitable diet.

At the end of the six-mile walk get someone to hold the dogs—sometimes this takes a bit of doing—and after showing them a piece of meat go on ahead for, say, two hundred yards, and then get the person holding them to let them go one at a time at intervals of ten to fifteen yards. This should be done twice, but not more, and not repeated more than twice a week at the start.

This training must be continued up to a fortnight before the chosen stake is due—*i.e.* six miles walking, the occasional bi-weekly gallop, and the massage. Once the stake is fixed up, and a fortnight only is left, the walk may be increased to eight miles, which is ample, and the gallops given daily and increased in length to a quarter of a mile at a stretch occasionally. Never overdo the dogs and get them stale, but rather than risk this, change the form of the gallop and give them a romp after a tennis ball. Variety is everything, but never overdo the gallops in any way. Always let the dog finish fresh, so that he feels he could do more if he were allowed. No real exercise must be given for two days before the meeting. Coincident with the change in exercise, the rhubarb pill should be repeated and the food gradually made drier. The bread should be toasted and broken up, and fed with the meat almost dry. Water, boiled, and changed night and morning, should of course always be in the dogs' kennels. As a change, cow-heels, boiled so that the cartilage falls off the bones, can be used, preferably being minced, mixed with the juice and then allowed to set solid so that it may be cut as a cake. Sheep's-head brawn, made in much the same way, is also relished, and a vegetable such as a well-boiled parsnip or an onion mixed with the food helps to make a change. During the last week a change should be made from horse-meat to mutton, as it is more digestible ; otherwise the feeding should remain the same until the day before the stake, when the last feed—preferably cow-heels, boiled, minced and caked—should be given not later than three o'clock in the afternoon, and the dog made comfortable and not disturbed until the next morning. The first thing on the day of the stake is to get him to open his bowels, and then, once this is done, he should be given half-a-teacupful of invalid Bovril, warm, and a slice of dry toast.

As soon as possible after this, he should be taken to the meet in whatever sort of covered conveyance can be procured. A cab with the windows whitewashed and a board placed over the seats makes quite a good one, but anything, so long as the dog can rest comfortably and not get excited by what is going on around him, will answer the purpose. On the day of the stake the dog's comfort is everything and the trainer must put up with what he can get. Just before the dog is due in the slips he should be taken

out and given a short walk and a rub down, and
then taken to slips. For the time being, the
training is over.

Supposing that a course is won, the dog should
be picked up as soon as possible, his mouth cleaned
of all fluff and hair and washed well out with
cold tea ; then he should be rubbed well down
with a mixture of equal parts Elliman's and olive
oil, and, after rugging him up, he should be put
back into the cab to sleep it off. Before he is
wanted again he should be given, about ten
minutes before, a good stiff dose of equal parts
port wine and Vibrona. This is much the best
and most easily digested stimulant. Then give
another good rubbing with Elliman's and olive
oil and take straight to the slips again.

This chapter, or these ideas, are certain to be
criticised, for two reasons : In the first place,
I do not recommend the length of walking exercise, on the road, that most authorities affirm
is necessary ; and, in the second place, I have
not mentioned the use of a horse in training.
My one idea throughout has been to put before
the novice a workable system of training that
can be applied by anyone who is a dog owner,
wherever he is and no matter what occupation
he earns his living by. I am of opinion, and
am certain I am right, that six miles fast road
work—that is to say, six miles covered in less than
one and a half hours—is far better for the dogs,

gets them fitter more quickly, and produces more stamina than a slow dawdle of twelve or fifteen miles. The six miles done at a swinging pace is just sufficient to brace the whole system up without the risk of the staleness or over-tiredness that longer walking is likely to produce. It is not a question of seeing how much a dog can do, but of getting him into such a condition that he is fit in himself to do his best.

Horse exercise I can see 'no advantage in, beyond the fact that it saves time in the galloping ; but though it may be useful and is always recommended, it can be easily dispensed with and is not one of the essentials of training.

SUMMARY OF TRAINING

	Exercise	Feeding	Massage
First fortnight	Six miles slow walking per day	Ordinary every-day food	Rub over
On until fortnight before stake	Six miles fast walking per day. Gallops of 200 to 300 yds. bi-weekly	Brown bread, meat, cow-heels, sheep's heads	Night and morning after exercise
Last fortnight	Six to eight miles fast walking per day. Gallops 200 to 300 yds. daily	Same diet, fed as dry as possible	...

IX

Feeding

THE rational feeding of any breed of animals is based on two or three fundamental facts which must be understood. In the first place, all foods are made up of three factors : proteids, or albuminoids ; carbohydrates, and fats. The proteids, or albuminoids, are complex substances made up of not only carbon, hydrogen and oxygen, but also of nitrogen and sulphur, and it is on account of their nitrogen content that they are so all-important a factor in the feeding. Nitrogen enters very largely into the composition of all muscle and bone tissue and can only be obtained from the proteins which are fed to the animal. The carbohydrates and fats contain no nitrogen, and when digested by the animal and passed into the body they are oxidised in the tissues with the production of carbonic acid gas and water, heat being given off during the process. In the body this heat is used by the animal for the maintenance of its proper warmth, and for the energy necessary for movement. Heat and energy are practically interchangeable. Over and above a certain point the excess of carbohydrates and fats is, after digestion, stored up in the liver and tissues of the body as sugar and fat.

From this it is obvious that the feeding of animals, in this case dogs, must be modified according as to what they are being prepared to do. In training, the maximum amount of protein with the bare necessity of carbohydrate must be fed, whilst in the brood bitch and growing puppy a greater proportion of carbohydrate and fat would not only be beneficial but advisable.

There are two other important factors—discoveries of very recent date — that must be considered. These are what are known as accessory food factors or vitamines. Of these there are two of importance at the moment and these are known as Fat Soluble A and Water Soluble B. The first of these factors is present chiefly in

(1) Certain fats of animal origin such as milk, butter, cod-liver oil, egg yolk, etc. ;
(2) Green leaves ;

but it is markedly deficient in, if not entirely absent from,

(1) Vegetable oils ;
(2) Root vegetables.

A great deal of experimental work has been done concerning these factors and it has been proved that, whilst Water Soluble B is necessary

HOPSACK, RUNNER-UP WATERLOO CUP, 1916

to promote the occurrence of growth, the Fat Soluble A factor is the all-important one, to us, as any deficiency in it is liable to cause rickets, which has been proved without a doubt to be due to this and nothing else.

As all the experiments were carried out on dogs the points brought out are interesting. In the first place, the substances which were fed and produced, or failed to prevent, rickets were white bread (*ad lib.*), oatmeal, rice, separated milk (*ad lib.*), calcium phosphate, sodium chloride and meat protein. This is remarkable as amongst the list are foods commonly used and often recommended by greyhound breeders, and substances such as calcium phosphate, which have often been advised as preventives. The report on these two substances reads :

" When a diet contains an excess of carbohydrate it means that it is made up largely of cereals. Now cereals, and more particularly cereals like wheat and rice, are most deficient in accessory food factors. A diet, therefore, of such substances is unbalanced and most effective in producing rickets."

And again :

" An abundance of calcium in the diet either in the form found in separated milk or as calcium phosphate will not prevent rickets when the diet is deficient in the anti-rachitic factor."

Now the substances which prevented rickets to a varying degree were as follow :—whole milk, cod-liver oil, butter, olive oil, suet, lard, meat and malt extracts.

These accessory food factors are not so important to the adult dog as to the growing puppy, but must be remembered.

From these points one can turn to a study of the foods usually fed, in a little more detail.

Meat : The relative composition of meat is

Foods of Animal Origin

	Proteins Per cent.	Fats Per cent.
Beef, neck	19·2	16·5
,, rump	16·8	25·6
Tripe	10·0	10·0
Mutton, neck	16·3	24·5
Horse, hind-quarter	21·6	3·1
,, breast	21·3	15·6

All meat is well supplied with Fat Soluble A and Water Soluble B.

From the above analysis it can easily be seen that, besides the advantage of cost, horse meat is infinitely preferable to either beef or mutton. The danger is, of course, the origin of the meat, but in these days, when every large city has one or more shops devoted to the sale of horse meat that has been passed as "fit for human consumption," there is not now the same risk as formerly.

As to how the meat is prepared is simply a

matter of personal likes or dislikes. Cooked meat is slightly less digestible than uncooked meat, but at the same time cooking has the advantage of developing the flavour and of destroying any parasites that may exist.

Personally, I think the best way is to cut up the meat into small pieces, place in a jar, cover with water, add a pinch of salt and allow it to simmer in an oven all day, never actually bringing it to a boil ; or, where a large kennel has to be fed, the meat should be cut up small in the same way and simmered in a boiler or Parrish's cooker. When this is done, a lot of the salts, albumen, proteids, etc., are dissolved out into the water, and whatever food is being used as a thickening agent should be soaked in this. This is easiest done if the meat is first removed, the bread or meal added, allowed to cool, and the meat returned to it. The smaller the pieces of meat and the longer the time of cooking, the poorer the meat becomes and the richer the broth, so that both must be used to obtain the full benefit.

In place of meat, sheep's heads or cow-heels may be used for a change. The former should be spilt and then simmered as previously described, whilst the latter must be boiled. Then the cartilage and tendon should be removed and passed, as it is, hot through the mincing machine and returned to the liquid. If the right amount of liquid has been used, the whole will set into a solid jelly, which is much relished and an excellent feed in the last stages of training. Brown bread, stale, can be minced and added to ensure setting, if desired.

Paunches and melts I do not approve and can see no use for.

Palates can be used in the same way as cow-heels and make an excellent feed, and bullock's cheek is a useful alternative to horse-meat.

Bones are more useful as an amusement for dogs than for any goodness they get out of them, but they must be free from splinters and of a large size. Chicken bones, rabbit bones, chop bones, etc., must on no account be used, as they splinter readily and the swallowing of a splinter often causes peritonitis and death.

Milk : For whelps, saplings and even puppies a certain amount of milk is ideal, but it is essential to remember the different compositions of the various milks.

	Water Per cent.	Butter Fat Per cent.	Sugar Per cent.	Casein Per cent.
Cow's Milk .	87·6	3·20	4·7	3·64
Bitch's Milk .	66·3	14·8	2·9	16·0
Goat's Milk .	84·94	5·14	5·28	4·06

Fat Soluble A is present in proportion to Butter Fat Content

From this it can be seen that bitch's milk is three times as strong as cow's milk or goat's milk —of which two the latter is the better, and if fed to whelps it must be strengthened by the addition of two ounces of cream, two ounces of Plasmon and five ounces of water to every half-pint of milk. The Plasmon must first be mixed with the water, then add the milk and boil slowly for two or three minutes ; allow to cool, and add the cream. Even this does not make up for the difference in the butter-fat contents entirely, and either cod-liver oil or Virol should be given in addition.

Milk, except for whelps at weaning time, is only used as an addition to the diet of an invalid or brood bitch, and in these cases I think goat's milk is excellent and far cheaper, if space for the goats is available, than cow's milk.

In cases where, for any reason, milk is difficult to get, I have had excellent results from the use of " Glaxo " full-cream milk powder, and think this is by far the best substitute on the market.

Eggs : The mere mention of these, with prices as they are, may seem ridiculous, but there are occasions when an egg will save a dog and then expense becomes a matter of minor consideration.

The composition is :

	Per cent.
Proteins .	12·6
Carbohydrates	0·6
Fats	12·1

Eggs are very rich in Fat Souble A.

Fish : The average constituents are

	Per cent.
Proteins .	18·2
Fats	7·1

Fish is almost entirely deficient in either of
the Accessory Food Factors.

From its constitution, fish is not of much
value as a food for dogs, but an occasional fish
meal makes a change and variety. It can be
bought as cods' heads, which should be put in
a large pan over a fire or in a boiler and boiled
hard until the flesh readily falls off the bones.
It must then be allowed to cool, the flesh removed and the liquid passed through a strainer to
remove the smaller bones. Meal or bread may
be soaked in the liquid and mixed with the flesh.

The dangers from the small bones are, in my
opinion, a very great contra-indication unless
great care is taken in their removal.

Cod Liver Oil : This is very rich in Fat
Soluble A and may with advantage be added to
the foods of whelps or given in teaspoonful doses
twice daily.

Foods of Vegetable Origin

	Protein Per cent.	Carbohydrates Per cent.	Fats Per cent.
Rice . .	7·8	79	0·4
Oatmeal .	15·6	68	7·3
Wheat Flour	11·8	75	1·1
Maize Meal .	7	66	4
Barley Meal .	8	48	4·3
Maize Germ Meal .	9	55	6·2

All these, with the exception of wheat flour, contain a certain amount of Fat Soluble A, whilst maize germ meal is particularly rich in it.

These farinaceous foods may all be used as ordinary everyday feeds for summering, brood bitches, or saplings, but the difficulty with all of them is the amount of cooking they require. For instance, oatmeal should be boiled for at least three hours and unless a large porridge boiler or a Parrish cooker is used there is great difficulty in preventing it burning. The easiest way, when using small quantities, is to tie one pound of Scotch oatmeal, four lumps of sugar and a lump of lard or dripping in a calico bag ; put this into a boiler with plenty of water, and it can be boiled as long as required without any risk of burning. When sufficiently boiled the cloth can be removed and the oatmeal strained and left to dry, when it can be cut like a cake. Fifty puddings of one pound each may easily be boiled in a large copper.

When using any of these meals, the danger of overheating must always be kept in mind, and plenty of vegetables such as cabbage, cauliflower, parsnips or onions used with them. Oatmeal is especially prone to overheat and cause rashes and eczema. Rice is very constipating ; maize meal very fattening and a poor food, and wheat flour a poor substitute at its best for stale wholemeal bread.

Potatoes chiefly consist of water, but when cooked in their skins contain a large amount of starch, and when fed occasionally they form an excellent alternative feed, especially during the last few weeks of training.

Fresh vegetables are hardly dog foods but they are very rich—the green-leafed ones—in vitamines, and given chopped in the feeds are useful in the preventive treatment of rickets.

Water : Water constitutes about half the live weight of dogs and is an indispensable component of all their tissues and secretions. I am convinced that water should always be in front of a dog, in a clean vessel, and should be changed night and morning ; also, if there is any doubt as to its source, it should be boiled before use.

X

Kennels

THE greyhound is usually considered to be a delicate dog, requiring artificial heat and specially constructed kennels, but if the three essentials of a good kennel—viz.

Absence of draught and damp ; possibility of warmth ; and good ventilation

are borne in mind, they will be found to be, within certain limits, as healthy or hardy as any other breed.

If no outbuildings exist and a kennel, or range of kennels, has to be purchased, such firms as Maggs, of Bristol ; Boulton & Paull, of Norwich ; or Penketh of Manchester make kennels specially designed for greyhounds. They should consist of an inside sleeping compartment about 6 ft. long by 6 ft. wide, connected by means of a door, which can be closed, with an outer run of about the same dimensions. The sleeping compartment must be floored and should have a bench 6 ft. long by 4 ft. wide raised 18 in. to 2 ft. from the floor and with a ledge six inches deep running the whole length of it.

This is preferably made so that it can be raised or lowered and should be made solid in front so that the dogs cannot creep underneath. Where room is an object and outbuildings scarce these kennels are excellent.

If, on the other hand, there are existing outbuildings available, these can be reconstructed to form ideal kennels. Some time back I had a ten-stall stable railed off into ten separate kennels, by means of 6-ft. iron railings and gates, in such a way that it was transformed into two rows of five kennels with a central passage between the rows. In the end of each stall, which was 12 ft. 6 in. from back to front, a wooden bench 6 ft. long by 4 ft. wide was fixed, with a ledge 6 in. high along its front edge, and the bench 18 in. off the ground. The flooring was of cobbles.

This formed an ideal greyhound kennel, easily cleaned out, easily heated, always dry and very convenient ; and it had the further advantage that the dogs saw each other, felt at home, and did not howl as greyhounds are apt to do when kennelled alone.

When outbuildings can be reconstructed, they form much more substantial and therefore warmer kennels than wooden ones and are preferable.

Heating : In the example given, the heat, when necessary, was obtained from an oil stove, but the better plan would be to run a 3-in.

pipe right round the walls, under the benches, and connect it up with an outside stove, on the same principle as the heating arrangements of a greenhouse.

Bedding : Straw is by far the best for this purpose, as hay is apt to sweat and cause rheumatism and kennel lameness. Shavings are also good, as, if of pine, they tend to prevent lice and fleas.

Litter : As the floors of outbuildings are usually of cobbles, bricks or asphalt, it is always advisable to use a litter of some sort, and there is nothing so good, for this, as pine sawdust, as it keeps down vermin, and is easily cleaned up.

Water : Movable water bowls should be fixed in each kennel and be cleaned and refilled night and morning. If the water is at all hard it is much better boiled before use.

Feeding Arrangements : A gas ring is essential for boiling water and warming separate lots of food, but for the main cooking a Parrish's Steam Cooker should be installed. These are excellent and have the great advantage that they can be left without any fear of the food burning.

Rugging : Kennel rugs are best of kersey cloth of the same material as horse rugs. These should be of different colours so that each dog has its own rug : this is important, as it obviates the risk of the transference of skin trouble from one dog to another. The outside exercising rugs should be of waterproof covert coating and lighter than the kennel rugging. All dogs must be rugged up during the training and coursing season, if necessary with two rugs, but should be left without them during the summer months.

Disinfecting : The litter from each kennel should be cleaned up night and morning and raked over, and the kennels themselves should be thoroughly cleaned out at least once a month. When this is done, the floors should be thoroughly scrubbed with either a strong solution of Jeyes' or Lysol, and fresh sawdust put down. The walls and benches should be whitewashed at least twice a year. Where many dogs are kept, it is a good plan to mix a strong solution of Jeyes' and place it in an old tin on the gas-ring and allow it to boil. The fumes given off act as a powerful deodoriser and clear the air of all noxious fumes and smells.

XI

Diseases

IN treating of the diseases of the greyhound, I intend to confine myself entirely to those which, I think, lie within the power of the owner, blessed with ordinary common sense, to diagnose and treat with some hope of success. I am no believer in either the amateur doctor or the amateur vet., and in any case of doubt or danger I am convinced that the one thing to be done is to obtain the help of a fully qualified, experienced member of whichever profession is required.

In the first place, there are one or two points concerning the examination of a sick dog that must be understood.

EXAMINATION

The Temperature : This is best taken by means of a half-minute clinical thermometer, obtainable at any chemist's.

The most convenient place in which to take it, in the dog, is the bowel. The dog should be held by an assistant and then, after well greasing the thermometer, the operator should take the dog between his legs, facing the tail, and after lifting the tail insert the thermometer for about an inch and a half, leaving it in place for at least a minute. If the assistant holds the dog by the collar and the operator controls him with his legs, there is not very much difficulty in the procedure.

In the dog, the normal temperature in the bowel, or rectum, is 101·4°. A temperature of anything above 103° or below 95° is dangerous and indicates serious trouble somewhere, especially if it is maintained.

It must be understood that a high or low temperature, like a good many other things— such as rapid or slow pulse, cough, rapid respiration, etc.—is only a symptom of a disease, and in any attempt to relieve it the rock-bottom cause of it must be diagnosed and treated. It is useless to treat symptoms and leave the cause untouched.

The Pulse : A dog's pulse, within limits, varies a great deal according to his size, but in the greyhound ranges round about a mean of 80 beats to the minute. It is best felt just inside the front of the hind leg, where the femoral artery crosses the thigh bone. In disease it is, as a rule, increased in frequency, often getting as fast as 120 beats per minute, but it may, on the other hand, slow down to as few as 50 per minute in some serious cases in which the heart is affected. Besides noting the number of beats to the minute, it is necessary to note, roughly, the strength of the pulse—as to whether it is strong or, as in long illnesses, weak and scarcely perceptible.

The Respirations : The normal number of respirations varies between 18 and 22 per minute, and in diseases accompanied by fever they are usually markedly increased, whereas in all serious affections of the brain, etc., and usually in distemper, the rate is lessened.

The Fæces or Stools : The shape, size, colour and consistency of the dog's motions often form an important point in the diagnosis of the disease. In normal health they are cylindrical in form and vary in consistency according to the nature of the food. As to colour : a dog on a meat diet has blackish stools, the same as one that is being dosed with calomel, bismuth or iron ; if the dog has eaten many bones they are whitish, whilst catarrh of the liver, or biliousness, will cause the stools to become yellow-coloured.

In regard to the consistency, this varies on either side of the normal, from diarrhœa to constipation. Both are symptoms of disease and must not be treated as true diseases.

Diarrhœa may be due to catarrh of the intestine caused by irregular diet, cold, distemper, septicæmia, or some of the irritant poisons such as iodine ; whilst constipation, which is common in old and debilitated dogs, is seen at the onset of fevers—such as distempter, obstruction of the bowels, worms, when present in large quantities, tumours, etc.

In regard to the size of the stools : a dog fed on a vegetable or bread diet passes a great deal more fæces than one fed on meat. In the former case the amount of fæces passed is equal to 20 per cent. of the food eaten, whilst in the latter case it only amounts to 12 per cent.

DISTEMPER

Definition : Distemper is an acute infectious disease affecting chiefly, but not solely, the dog, and characterised by high temperature, depression, loss of appetite and the implication of one or other, or several, of the various systems of the body.

Etiology : Various observers have, from time to time, announced the discovery of the causal organism of the disease, but nothing very satisfactory was done until, in 1910, Ferry isolated a bacterium—a short, narrow bacillus—which he named the bacillus broncho-septicus and which he considered to be the causal organism of the disease. His discovery has been corroborated by several other observers, notably M'Gowan, Torrey and Rahe, and it is now generally recognised.

Diseases

Symptoms : The period of incubation ranges from seven to eight days, and the first actual symptom is a rise in temperature, which goes up to between 104° and 105°. The next symptom is the disturbance of the general condition. The dog is obviously depressed, has no appetite, is shivering, retires to the darkest and warmest corner of its kennel, the nose is hot and dry and, as often as not, there is vomiting and diarrhœa. This stage lasts from twenty-four to forty-eight hours and the symptoms then develop in one of four characteristic forms, which are as follow :—

(1) Catarrhal distemper, which is best defined as a " distemper " affecting the mucous membranes of the eyes, nose and lungs.

(2) Abdominal distemper, or a " distemper " affecting the mucous membranes of the whole intestinal tract, stomach and intestines.

(3) Cerebral distemper, or a " distemper " affecting the coverings—the meninges—of the brain and spinal cord.

(4) Rash distemper, or a " distemper " accompanied by a rash on the under parts of the abdomen and the inside of the thighs.

(1) *Catarrhal Distemper* : In this form there is a discharge of pus and mucus from the nose and eyes, accompanied by a cough. If the disease can be arrested at this stage the whole syndrome is really very similar to an attack of

influenza, but if it extends it first involves the larynx, or voice box, and then gradually extends to the mucous membranes of the tubes of the lung — the bronchi — until the smaller tubes become affected and a pneumonia results. This is evidenced by irregularity and increased frequency of the breathing—60 to 80 or more ; a remittent, or up and down, temperature ; a very rapid pulse, and a dry, hard, painful cough. On listening to the chest, snoring, wheezing and groaning sounds can be heard, together with rattles and blowing noises.

The eyes in the early stages are slightly affected, the dog avoids the light, there is swelling and redness of the conjunctiva, the excretion, which is at first watery, becomes purulent and runs out on to the cheek, drying on the face and frequently sticking the lids together. If this is not carefully attended to, the cornea, or front of the eye, becomes affected ; an ulcer results and, as a rule, the sight is badly affected, if not, indeed, lost.

(2) *Abdominal Distemper* : Often known as Stuttgart's distemper, this is chiefly characterised by vomiting and diarrhœa, which vary in intensity. The appetite is lost and the dog vomits quantities of thin, glairy fluid and passes motions of the same consistency, sometimes streaked with blood. The abdomen is frequently distended and tender, and there is very often

jaundice—shown by the yellow coloration of the whites of the eyes.

(3) *Cerebral Distemper* : This is the most dreaded form and is characterised by symptoms pointing to irritation and then paralysis of the brain. Twitchings of the muscles of the face are common. These may be followed by twitchings of the muscles of the legs, to be followed in turn by paralysis. The dog gradually becomes unable to stand, and the bowels and bladder are emptied involuntarily.

(4) *Rash Distemper* : This is characterised by the appearance of a rash consisting of small red spots on the under surface of the abdomen and the inner surface of the thighs. Gradually these spots form small blisters, which exude pus and then dry up with the formation of scabs. There is a peculiar and characteristic smell with this form.

Course : Distemper usually runs its course in from fourteen days to three weeks—that is, unless secondary complications, such as pneumonia, intervene.

After Effects : Deafness, blindness, sterility, St Vitus's dance, loss of sense of smell, paralysis of hind legs, etc., are all due to secondary complications, indicating the spread of the disease to other parts and the lodgment of bacteria, or their toxins, there.

Treatment : No one drug has been found to

date that has the property of destroying or rendering harmless the causal micro-organism of this disease. The whole aim of treatment must be directed to keeping the dog warm, preventing the further spread of the disease, and to keeping the heart going by means of stimulants.

The use of drugs for reducing the temperature is objectionable, as by doing this one of the best guides to the course of the disease is lost, and, moreover, drugs that reduce the temperature almost invariably depress the heart and this must at all costs be avoided. The dog must be kept warm, and this is, to my mind, best done by placing a good layer of Thermogene wool between the rug and the skin. This acts in much the same way, only without its disadvantages, as a poultice, and ensures warmth in the region of the lungs. In cases where it is impossible to artificially heat the kennels by hot-water pipes, etc., resource must be had to oil-stoves or hot-water bottles and, where it is feasible to make use of the first-named alternative, a little oil of creosote placed in a tin on the top of the stove not only disinfects the kennel by its fumes but has a distinctly beneficial effect on the catarrhal conditions.

The eyes must be attended to regularly and from the onset of the disease must be treated at least twice a day. The best treatment is to first drop into each eye, by means of a glass fountain-pen filler, one drop of a 10 per cent. solution of argyrol, and then, after allowing this to remain in for five minutes, wash out with a weak solution of

℞
Boric Acid
a teaspoonful to the pint

or

℞
Sulphate of Zinc
one grain to the ounce

After this has been done, the lids should be thoroughly dried and then smeared with a little

℞
Ung. Hydrarg. Oxid. Flav.

On no account should patent ointments, such as Golden Ointment, be used.

For the vomiting and diarrhœa there is nothing, in my opinion, so good as

℞
Bisedia (Schatt)
in teaspoonful doses night and morning

As to the diet, it is necessary that whatever is given be highly nutritious and easily digested. Scraped raw meat, milk, eggs, Brand's Chicken Essence, mutton broth, are all excellent, and a further stimulant can be given :

℞

Brandy	.	.	.	.	1 tablespoonful
Water	.	.	.	.	2 tablespoonfuls
White of egg					

Mix the white of egg with the water (do not whip), and then add the brandy. Use night and morning.

Or again :

℞

Brandy	.	.	.	1 tablespoonful
Virol	.	.	.	1 teaspoonful
Milk	.	.	.	1 tablespoonful

used in the same way

Personally, I prefer drenching with these small quantities to giving nutrients by the rectum, as even when all else fails either of the two suggested will keep a dog going long enough to turn the corner. If he will eat voluntarily so much the better, but the action of the heart must be maintained by stimulant all through, and the best to use is undoubtedly brandy.

Preventive Inoculation against Distemper : At the present time, when serum and vaccine therapy form so important a part in the treatment of diseases of the human subject, it seems extraordinary that prophylactic vaccination against distemper has not become more generally adopted. The theory, and rationale, of the treatment is identically the same, and yet, whilst it is almost universally adopted in infectious diseases of the human being, it is still looked at askance when mentioned in connection with distemper and the dog.

The theory, in brief, of serum and vaccine therapy is as follows :—When a microbe, bacterium, or bacillus gains entry into the body it settles there and rapidly multiplies, and at the same time produces poisonous substances known as toxins. Now the body, or rather the blood in it, reacts to this microbe or its toxins in one of two ways : In the first place, in the blood, in addition to the red blood corpuscles, there are white blood corpuscles, which, when the microbe settles, become enormously increased in number. These white corpuscles act really as the scavengers of the body, and have the power of ingesting and digesting foreign substances such as bacteria, but the bacteria must be prepared, or " sensitised," by another substance, produced in the blood, before the white blood corpuscles can act upon them. This special substance is produced separately for each bacterium, and the idea of vaccine therapy, on this method, is that by injecting weak or attenuated bacteria, in the form of vaccines, this special substance is produced in sufficient quantity in advance, so that when the bacterium actually does come along the substance is there and the white blood corpuscles have not to wait while it is being formed but can go straight on with the work of eating up the bacteria. This is known as phagocytosis.

The second theory is slightly more complicated, as two substances are necessary, and of these the first is what is known as the amboceptor. This may occur normally in the blood, but is produced to excess when the stimulating factor, the antigen, is injected into the tissues.

The second substance is known as the complement and is invariably present in the blood. In itself it is without action on bacteria, but when these have been attacked by the amboceptor the complement comes along and does the rest. Put shortly, the amboceptor unites with the bacteria and renders it vulnerable to the complement, which digests it. The theory of vaccines in this case is practically identical. The amboceptors are not produced in any quantity until they are excited by the particular bacteria they are wanted for, so that the idea is the same as in the first way, to have the amboceptors ready before the actual bacteria come along.

Practically speaking, the human being or animal is given a mild attack of the disease, which helps to the acquirement of a resisting power against the more virulent variety.

Possibly much of the controversy on this subject—vaccination against distemper—has arisen because the vaccines have not been carefully enough made and the right organism has not been isolated. The amboceptors in the one case or the substance in the blood in the other case that are necessary for the attack on the distemper bacteria cannot be produced by the injection of any other attenuated bacteria than those of distemper. This applies in exactly the same way as in the human being. An injection of anti-typhoid vaccine or serum would have no effect in the prevention of diphtheria, or vice versa. This point is apt to be overlooked.

Personally, I made a thorough trial of preventive inoculation in connection with exhibition dogs and saw no bad effects of any kind that could possibly be attributed to the injections, and, further, never had, nor have I seen, a case of distemper in a properly vaccinated animal.

There are several anti-distemper vaccines on the market, and of these I think the best are : " Malfin," prepared under the supervision of a medical man with a big kennel of his own ; Dr Copeman's, prepared by the Jenner Institute ; and that put on the market by Messrs Parke Davis, of London.

The technique of the injection is simple. The skin over the muscles of the shoulder is sterilised by being painted with tincture of iodine. A hypodermic syringe is sterilised by immersion in absolute alcohol : this is then washed out with a little boiled water. The syringe is filled with the vaccine, the needle is attached and then inserted deeply into the muscles of the shoulder. The vaccine is then injected and the syringe and needle removed. The place of entry of the needle is again dabbed over with iodine.

The dog may be seedy or go off its feed for a day or so, but in the majority of cases I have seen there has been no reaction whatever and the dog has eaten and exercised as usual.

ECZEMA AND MANGE

Under this heading a great variety of diseases are included, varying from blotch to mange. Their causes, like their varieties, are many, and the treatment, naturally, depends upon the cause.

Eczema : To take true eczema first : This is a cutaneous disease common to all breeds of dogs, *it is not contagious*, and is an inflammatory condition of the skin, denoted as a rule by redness and intense irritation either in one patch or in a diffuse and widely distributed form. From these patches, or areas, there is an exudation.

If these cases are treated in time the disease stops at this stage, but if they are allowed to go on, the irritation increases and small red, raised, rough nodules are formed, which break down and form small sores with a great deal of exudation and scab formation. The exudation dries rapidly and the scabs form at once, and when they fall off bare patches are left. There is not, as a rule, great infiltration of the skin.

The first thing to do, in cases of this description, is to attempt to discover the cause. It may quite likely be due to worms, and if so nothing will have any effect upon the skin condition until these are removed. Then again, fleas, lice, tick and sheep nits are all common causes, and if discovered should at once be treated and removed. I am no great believer in the treatment of greyhounds by means of baths and I think the most efficacious way to treat these pests is to rub the dogs thoroughly all over with a lotion.

℞

Olive Oil ⎫
Paraffin ⎭ . . Of each equal parts

None of the animal pests can exist without air, and the object of this lotion is to remove all air by the paraffin, which is more or less, according to its quality, volatile, and then to exclude more by means of the olive oil.

Another frequent cause is feeding with overheating food, such as porridge, and this condition is often seen in greyhounds that have been badly summered, or fed too highly, during training, with insufficient exercise. The name "blotch," by which it is commonly known, is very descriptive. For this, I think a course of

℞ Benbow's Mixture

is excellent, or another good tonic is Fowler's solution, but this must be used with care, as arsenic is not an ideal drug to use indiscriminately. The diet must be modified, heating food omitted, and the bowels kept loose by either saline purgatives or vegetables.

Another cause, during the winter, is the indiscriminate use of water on the legs and feet.

The dogs come in hot from exercise; warm water is not to hand, so cold, often icy cold, hard water is used to remove the mud. This chills the skin and at once produces an inflammation and an eczema similar to the "mud rash" of horses. The less water used on greyhounds in the winter the better, and it is a far better practice to let the legs and feet get thoroughly dry, with the mud on them, and then remove it by means of a brush or clean, fine sawdust, than to risk water. Eczema, once started, is a nuisance to stop. Ointments such as

R

Glycola (Clarke's)

R

Cold Cream

R

Witch Hazel

R

Hazeline

are all useful, but prevention is a very much more satisfactory treatment than cure and the disease should be obviated by every possible care.

These true eczemas can be distinguished from the real manges by the following facts :—

(1) Mange is produced by definite parasites.

(2) It occurs in situations favoured by those parasites.

(3) It invariably appears in single spots and it is only after it has been left untreated for some sime that these spots coalesce.

(4) A microscopical examination of the hair or scales of the skin will always furnish a definite diagnosis.

Diseases

The manges are of two main forms :

    (1) Sarcoptic Mange
    (2) Follicular Mange

Sarcoptic Mange (Red Mange) is caused by the sarcoptes scabiei squamiferis, which burrows in the skin and after forming pustules and raised areas gradually causes a secondary inflammation producing thickening of the entire depth of the skin, causing it to be thrown into folds and wrinkles, with the formation of ulcers and sores in the intervening furrows.

This is the most contagious form of mange, but, at the same time, it is the most curable. It may be distinguished from follicular mange by the general appearance and also from the fact that in the latter there is little, if any, irritation. A dog with raised pustules, skin in folds, and who immediately starts to scratch if his back is rubbed, can be diagnosed as a case of sarcoptic mange.

The treatment consists of first getting the dog thoroughly clean by means of a bath and the free application of either soft or liquid soap ; then he must be rubbed all over with one of the following ointments and liniments :—

℞

    Picis liquida
    Sapo. Pot. virid. }   .   of each equal parts
    Spiritus Vini Rect.

181

or

℞

Lysol					
Sapo. Pot. virid. }	.	.	of each one part
Sp. Vin. Rect.	.	.	ten parts

or

℞

Ol. Cade	.	.	.	.	.	1 oz.
Præcip. sulphur	.	.	.	.	3 oz.
Ol. Olivæ	.	.	.	.	1 pint

or

℞

Beta Naphthol	.	.	.	.	1 drachm
Sulphur præcip.	.	.	.	.	2 ,,
Storax	.	.	.	.	.	6 ,,
Pulv. Pyrethrum	.	.	.	6 ,,
Lard	.	.	.	.	.	3 oz.

These must in each case be thoroughly rubbed in and left for three days ; then the dog should be bathed, using coal tar soap, and then whichever treatment has been chosen should be used again and, after being left on for a further three days, finally washed off. In most cases this treatment will effect a cure, but at the least sign of a recurrence it must be repeated.

Follicular Mange (Black Mange) is caused by a parasite known as *acarus demodese folliculorum.* The features of the disease are the black coloration of the skin, the absence of irritation and the presence of the parasite in the hairs. It is extremely difficult, if not impossible, to cure and, unless the dog is a particularly valuable one, the best treatment is to destroy him, once the diagnosis has been confirmed by microscopical examination.

In both varieties of mange the dogs must be isolated and, when cured, all bedding, rugs, etc. must be burnt, and the whole kennel thoroughly limewashed and disinfected. It is of no use curing a dog of mange and then putting on an old rug that has been merely sterilised by washing. Better burn the old rug and buy a new one ; it is less expensive in the long run.

Enteritis (*Inflammation of the Bowels*)

This disease is characterised by frequent watery motions, often accompanied by pain and straining.

The cause must be sought for and treated. This may be worms, irregular feeding, insufficient exercise, or one of the poisons such as iodine.

Once the cause has been discovered and removed, the following may be useful :—

℞

Brandy	.	.	.	.	1 tablespoonful
Water	.	.	.	.	2 tablespoonfuls
White of egg					

Mix the white of egg with the water (do not whip), and then add the brandy. The dose is a dessertspoonful every two hours, and the dog should be fed on finely minced raw horse-meat and given barley water (Robinson's) in place of water.

Epilepsy

Epileptic fits are not common in dogs unless

following upon the convulsions or fits of distemper or worms.

The only treatment is, I think, to destroy the dog, as nothing can do any lasting good.

FRACTURES AND DISLOCATIONS

These are of so many possible varieties that they cannot come into the scope of this book, besides which they are in the domain of a veterinary surgeon, and one, moreover, who makes dogs his speciality.

LARYNGITIS

In greyhounds, especially in puppies, this affection very often occurs after a meeting. The most common cause is undoubtedly the pressure of the slips upon the larynx whilst the dog is making efforts to get to his game. It is evidenced by a hoarse, harsh, dry, raucous cough, almost a bark, which is incessant and very annoying. It is best treated by

℞

Glycoheroin
one teaspoonful night and morning

two days' treatment with which is usually sufficient to cure the trouble.

MUSCULAR RHEUMATISM

Rheumatism sometimes occurs when dogs are brought in from exercise overheated and then allowed to lie about and chill. The muscles of the back and loin are those usually affected.

If dogs are exercised in thinner sheets than they are kennelled in, and rubbed well down on returning from exercise, this trouble will very seldom occur. Covert-coating rugs are by far the best for exercising, as not only are they waterproof but they are thin and warm, and if, when the dogs return from exercise, these are changed for kennel rugs of thick kersey cloth, it is much better than attempting to rely upon one set of rugs to do duty in the dual capacity.

If rheumatism does occur, the dog should be treated with

℞

    Aspirin, ...   gr. v.
              one tablet night and morning

and the affected muscles well rubbed with either

℞

    Lin. Sap. Co.

or

℞

   Elliman's Embrocation }
   Olive Oil   } Of each equal parts

RICKETS

Now that the cause of this very troublesome disease has been definitely discovered to be due to a deficiency in one of the accessory food factors—Fat Soluble A—it is probable that cases will become less and less frequent, until eventually it becomes a rare disease.

I have taken up the preventive measures in other chapters and need only repeat that Fat Soluble A is chiefly present in

(1) Green Leaves
(2) Animal Oils

and is markedly deficient in root vegetables and vegetable oils. Butter or butter fat is the richest of all in this factor, and bitch's milk contains at least 14 per cent. of butter-fat. It is therefore obvious that when puppies are weaned this fact must be kept continually in mind and the lack of butter-fat made up by adding cream, lard, cod-liver oil or Virol to the dietary.

Once established, the disease is very difficult to cure, and at the best only partial success can be hoped for.

Cod liver oil, Virol, Parrish's Food, etc. are all useful, but it is eminently a disease for preventive measures rather than for cure.

Worms

These may be divided into :

Nematoda, or round worms ;
Cestoda, or tape-worms.

Every puppy born suffers, more or less, from round worms, and a great proportion of older dogs from tape-worm. It follows, then, that all dogs should be treated for round worms as soon as they are weaned. There are many excellent remedies, but from a very extensive experience I have come to rely upon

℞

Ruby (Nicholas)

as the best of them. In older dogs a prescription such as the following :—

℞

Areca Nut	.	.	.	.	2 oz.
Kamala	.	.	.	.	1 oz.
Santonin	.	.	.	.	2 dr.
Pulv. Lic. Co.	.	.	.	½ oz.

Mix and divide into fifteen powders. One powder to be given after eighteen hours' fasting.

For tape-worm the above prescriptions are good, but when more drastic measures are required

℞

| Santonin | . | . | . | . | gr. viii. |
| Castor Oil | . | . | . | . | 1 oz. |

or

℞

Thymol	.	.	.	.	grs. v.
Sp. Vin. Rect.	.	.	.	½ oz.
Castor Oil	.	.	.	.	1 oz.

are useful. The great thing in either is to give the medicine after fasting, and an additional help is to give a large dose of salts about an hour before giving the worm medicine. This clears out the water from the intestines and

gives the powder or medicine a better chance
to get at the worms.

Wounds

All wounds are accompanied by three
symptoms :

(1) The open, gaping condition of the edges.
(2) Hæmorrhage.
(3) Pain.

As a general rule, the wider the wound the
deeper it is. If the wound is in the direction
of the muscles it does not gape, but if it is
across them their retraction causes a great deal
of gaping.

The hæmorrhage may be either arterial, venous,
or capillary. The danger of arterial bleeding
depends entirely on the size of the artery which
has been cut and also upon the direction of the
cut. An oblique cut bleeds more freely and
for a longer period than a clean, sharp, trans-
verse cut. Venous bleeding, except in the case
of large veins, is not important, and can usually
be controlled by pressure, and capillary bleeding
comes into the same category.

In cases of severe hæmorrhage the dog goes
cold in the extremities ; the mucous membranes
become pale, especially those of the mouth and
eyes ; there is great prostration, staggering gait
and often an inability to rise at all. The pulse

becomes very weak and rapid, and if the bleeding continues the dog becomes unconscious and dies. Dogs can lose at least one quarter of the total amount of blood in their bodies and yet recover.

The pain of the wounds varies with the character of the dog and the situation of the wound. A greyhound cries out more quickly with pain than a bull-terrier. Wounds involving the bones, genital organs and face are the most painful.

Treatment : The treatment of wounds must be studied under three headings :

(1) Disinfection of the Wound.
(2) Arrest of Hæmorrhage.
(3) Alleviation of Pain.

Disinfection of Wounds : The whole aim of this must be to destroy, or wash out, the infective organisms present in the wound and further to prevent the entrance of other organisms into it.

In all large wounds, and if possible in small ones, the hair around the wound should be shaved very close and the skin washed with benzine to remove the fat from it. Then it should be thoroughly washed with

℞

Lysol
a teaspoonful to a pint of water

or

℞

Jeyes' Fluid
a teaspoonful to a pint of water

A thorough drenching is better than a dabbing with the lotion on cotton wool, as the latter is apt to rub the bacteria in whilst the former mechanically washes them away.

When this has been done the hæmorrhage must be arrested. In mild cases this can be done by pressure, but in cases where there is a deep-cut gaping wound it is better done by means of stitches. An ordinary sewing needle threaded with silk will answer the purpose in an emergency. Both must be sterilised by inserting them in boiling water. The needle should then be passed deeply into the tissues, wide of the edge of the wound, then under the base of the wound and out at the other side wide of the edge. This takes up a lot of tissue but, by tightening the ligature, brings the edges into apposition and stops the hæmorrhage.

In cases of very severe bleeding supervening on an injury to a big artery in one of the limbs, the best method of arresting it is to bandage the limb higher up than the bleeding point—*i.e.* nearer the body—and then, if possible, catch the bleeding point with a pair of artery forceps and tie it with a silk ligature. This latter is rather outside the province of the novice, but if the hæmorrhage is arrested by the bandage there is ample time to get a veterinary surgeon to complete the operation.

Hæmorrhage must be definitely arrested before

any attempt at dressing the wound is made, as blood clot is one of the most favourable media for the development of suppuration and the risks of septicæmia, pyæmia, etc.

In small wounds, where the hæmorrhage has been arrested and the edges brought into apposition, the simplest means of protection is to paint over with collodion or the proprietary "New Skin." This must be painted on and allowed to dry.

Larger wounds must be protected by gauze dressings and bandages, and care must be taken that the latter are not applied too tightly.

Ulcers : When the wound does not heal up by first intention—that is to say, edge to edge—but gapes and appears to heal from the bottom with a granulating surface, great care must be taken to keep the surface clean by frequent douchings with lotion. Then it must be carefully dried with cotton-wool dabs and dusted with one of the antiseptic powders, such as bismuth subnitrate, orthoform, etc. Iodoform should not be used, as it often causes symptoms of poisoning. In the event of proud flesh springing up, it should be touched with the caustic stick and then treated as before.

Some Useful Prescriptions

In every kennel a certain amount of drugs should be kept in case of urgent need. The following is a fair working list, which can, of course, be added to :—

Artery Forceps
Scissors
Bandages
Gauze
Lint
Cotton Wool
Needles, Half-curved surgical
Cotton
Silk-worm Gut (black, as it is more easily seen)
Iodine
Lysol
Jeyes' Fluid
Caustic Stick

℞

Castor Oil

℞

Castor Oil ⎫
Syrup of Buckthorn ⎭ . each equal parts

A tablespoonful three days before whelping. This is not so drastic as the pure oil.

℞

Bisedia (Schatt)

One teaspoonful twice daily. Very useful in cases of persistent diarrhœa and vomiting after cause has been removed.

℞

Pulv. Rhei Co. . gr. v. in tablets or tabloids
One at night

Very useful as a general liver corrective. Often used in course of training.

Diseases

℞

Ruby (Nicholas)

For worms. Directions accompany it.

℞

Benbow's Mixture

Very useful occasionally during training.

℞

Virol

Always useful for out-of-sorts dogs or weak puppies.

℞

Glaxo, Full Cream

A good substitute for milk.

℞

Ol. Cade	. . . . .	1 oz.
Præcip. sulphur	. . . .	3 oz.
Olive Oil	. . . . .	1 pint.

To be rubbed on at first sign of skin trouble.

℞

Paraffin ⎱
Ol. Olive ⎰ . . . each equal parts.

To be rubbed on for lice, etc.

XII

Coursing in Ireland

By W. H. TWAMLEY, *Official Slip Steward
to the Irish Coursing Club*

COURSING in Ireland is no doubt a very ancient field sport. The emblematic figure of Erin is accompanied by her hound in many a pictorial illustration, and though the hound is usually more like a deerhound, dogs of this rough-haired type are still to be seen in this country, and are registered as pure greyhounds in the *Greyhound Stud Book*. Some I have seen and known myself, and one good bitch who was a frequent winner some years back was clipped when in training, and running, by a horse-clipping machine.

Probably no country in the world can equal Ireland in suitable arenas for public open coursing, with its profusion of broad and extensive grassy plains. In many cases the land purchase Acts of Parliament have been the means of altering the proprietors, as the wealthy landlord who kept game on his own property unmolested, because of his strict preservation and gamekeepers, has passed out of ownership and now the

HONEYMAN, RUNNER-UP WATERLOO CUP, 1921

many smaller farmers are the owners; as a consequence there is no preservation and the supply of hares does not exist. Bourbawn, Lurgan, Toombridge, Dunlavin, Black Brea, Dunsandle, Kilwaunock, etc., were all the best Irish coursing grounds even in my time and are now *non est.* Then, as these meetings one by one passed away, lovers of coursing in any shape had recourse to the only other alternative—viz. to run caught and penned hares. Very often this sort of coursing was most undesirable, and the development of clubs and grounds with trained hares and proper escapes was adopted and now we have many excellent fixtures on this system. Those most prominent at present are Limerick, Cork, Maryborough, Masserene, Kilmannock, Kilteely, Ardee, Ardpatrick, Enniscorthy, Tralee, Dundalk, Nenagh, Mooncoin, Tuam, etc. At these meetings there is usually a very large attendance and the sport is now exceedingly popular, but the majority of its patrons are what would be called across the Channel "small men." Big kennels are not common, and the Irish aristocracy hold off, unfortunately, preferring the sister sport of fox-hunting.

Ireland has produced in recent years many good greyhounds. Of course the immortal Master M'Grath was an Irish dog, and we look forward to many more high-class performers being bred in the near future, as Ireland now

possesses stud dogs and brood bitches of the very
best lines of blood, and every care is taken in
bringing them up and training, etc.

In the season 1905–1906 the Irish Cup was
inaugurated at Clounanna, Co. Limerick. At
first it was not confined to any arena, as the
Creagh and Co. Wexford and Tralee were the
scenes of the competitions. Wexford Stob-
lands and the Creagh are meadows of the Altcar
type, but Tralee was run on the race-course, a
park meeting essentially. Only last year the
Maryborough Queen's County Club came into
existence, and its popularity and success have been
most remarkable from the first. This year they
will hold a Midland Cup meeting to somewhat
replace the Irish Cup, which it is impossible to
run at Limerick because of the now unsettled
political condition of most of the south of
Ireland.

As to the breeding of the greyhounds now
running in Ireland, because of the very numerous
importations of greyhounds of the best English
blood, purchased mostly at Messrs Stollerys'
London Barbican Sales, the blood of the great
majority of Irish public running greyhounds is
identical with that in the best English kennels.
Dogs of Messrs Fawcetts' strains have been bred
from, and also imported as sires from time to
time. In recent years perhaps the purchase of
the great dog Harmonicon was the most im-

portant and his success as a sire is phenomenal. Let 'Im Out, from the Duke of Leeds' kennels, is another case in point, though the Duke sold him in early war years for a bagatelle. Another Waterloo winner we had here as sire for a short time was Hoprend. It was in Ireland the good dog Hopsack was sired. Glenbridge, a Waterloo Cup runner-up, and Full Steam, also second for the big event, were located in this country, though neither was as well patronised as they deserved ; but Mr M. Hearne, of Dublin, always liked to possess a good sire, and his lucky purchases of the Netherby Cup winner, Spytfontein, and the extra-well-bred Fight for Freedom and Topsman did much for the improvement of Irish greyhounds in recent years, and their blood is still running in the present-day best greyhounds now running. Looking further back, we had the very fast and good-looking dog Alec Halliday, a Gosforth Park £1000 Cup winner, in this country. His successful progeny were not numerous. Why, I cannot say. The late Mr Frank Watson, of Lurgan, and Mr S. S. Swinburne, of Dublin, had kennels often occupied by good greyhounds. Years back the latter gentleman had a most successful pair of sires in Gone and Surprise, the latter an Irish-bred dog who ran up for the Waterloo Cup in Magnano's year. In the year 1878 the recently deceased nobleman, Lord Fermoy, ran up for the

The Greyhound & Coursing

Waterloo Cup with a smart bitch, Zazel, and only last year Mr M. L. Hearne was in the same position with the smart dog Honeyman, whose defeat in the final at Altcar has been so much discussed since, as many good judges believe he never should have had the flag against him then, as Fighting Force did nothing with the hare when the Irish dog turned back, being intimidated by the yelling crowd. Mr Hearne ascribes this dog's timidity to his being so near an aerodrome at Clondalkin. The constant humming of the aeroplanes overhead were a source of terror to this dog as a sapling, as they passed over the country flying low in the neighbourhood where he was in his earlier days.

There is little doubt that the future of Coursing in Ireland is bright in the extreme, when this unhappy country emerges from the clouds of gloom at present hanging over it. I believe that at present there are many more greyhounds in Ireland than in England and Scotland put together. The want of guns, which are all taken up now, will help the increase of hares, which are more numerous than ever at present.

Our well-known judge, Mr Maurice Davin, has held some sales of greyhounds that have been quite successful : many excellent greyhounds have passed through his sale rings to the benefit of their new possessors. In no part of the world is there a better place than Ireland to rear and bring up saplings, as both oatmeal and milk are in plenty amongst the farming population.

An ancient form of coursing is practised in the south (Co. Cork especially), where large tracts of the country are well preserved by the farmers and peasant proprietors. The young men gather after Sunday devotions and course most of the day. Dogs are put in slips, but a judge is not often engaged—each one is his own judge. Sometimes over a hundred dogs will be drawn for a stake and it will be run for Sunday after Sunday until run off. The hares are extra good and strong and not many are killed. Personally I have never been present at such gatherings.

I have as a coursing judge for years seen coursing in every part of Ireland, and a few personal incidents may be not without interest to the readers. At Mullingar one day a fine black dog was running well, but before being caught up he saw in the distance a hare, which he pursued, and in jumping a great water ditch broke his neck. His owner carried the dog some distance to a gap through which the crowd was passing on a change of heat. The man sat on the ground, showing all who passed by the disjointed neck of his favourite, and as I rode through he shouted for me to hear : " Judge, I'd sooner my mother had broken her neck than

the dog!" Then on another occasion I have
seen over a thousand men follow the hare and
hounds for a couple of miles over a wide expanse
of mossy turf bog—they had mixed up coursing
with a harrier hunt, and were with difficulty
restrained, to finish the day's coursing.

At a Midland meeting one day I was mounted
on a broken-down race-horse; his galloping days
were well past and every step seemed to be the
last. The hare took her pursuers in one course
through a wide and deep slough of black mud
and water. Thinking only of the course that
was being run, I put my sorry steed through
the morass, when about in the middle my
"mount" stood on his head and sent me sprawl-
ing into the mire. With plenty in my eyes
and mouth, kind helpers scraped my scarlet coat
and I was little the worse.

I was another time engaged to judge a fixture
in the Wild West. Some short time previous
to my going there I was accosted by a burly
farmer, who said : " Are you going to ——? " I
said : " I hope so." " Well," said he, " be sure
to have your will made, and affairs settled, as if
one dog that will be there does not win it is
more than likely you will go home in a wooden
suit with brass buttons." " What have I done
to earn such a fate? " " Nothing," said he,
" except that this dog *must* win again. At the last
meeting he won there and festivities were kept

THE SLUICE AT BALLYBEGGAN PARK

AN ESCAPE AT CLOUNANNA

up for some time after the event, and the whole
country-side are looking forward to a repetition."
Well, when we came to the running a big fawn
dog won easily his first course. On the hoisting
of the flag in his favour cheers, yells, hurrahs
rent the heavens ; hats and sticks were thrown
into the air. "This is the dog I must look after,"
said I to myself. He won again all right, and
again the uproar took place. When slipped for
his third course a gallant hare took him and
his opponent through many a field and meadow,
and the dog was quite exhausted, so that when
slipped again he was unable to raise a gallop,
and when the flag went up against him a silence
that could be felt prevailed, so I escaped from
any blame. What would have occurred had he
been beaten in a "near thing" I dare not say.

I have also been at a meeting where the
"public" were penned up in barbed-wire
entanglements, the only place to keep them off
the running ground and from following dogs
and hares wherever they went. The Irish are
wonderfully enthusiastic in sport, as may be
known at Liverpool if an Irish horse wins the
Grand National race.

Some writers have endeavoured to throw
slurs and doubts on the enclosed system of
coursing. In my opinion it has been the only
means of keeping the sport alive in this country.
The present enclosures are a wonderful improve-

ment on releasing caught hares on unknown grounds, to run on until they were killed or they killed their pursuers. This was very cruel and quite unsportsmanlike.

English coursers may not all know that Irish hares and English hares are not identical, nor do they run alike. The English hares often run much more twistily and require cleverer greyhounds. I think the Irish hare is the same as the Scotch blue hare on the mountains. The two varieties do not interbreed.

Before concluding this chapter I would like to say a few words on the rearing of saplings. There are several *musts* that will be absolutely necessary. To have good dogs, unlimited exercise and freedom from worms are essential, as well as the best of blood, but especially aim at winning strains on the dam's side and a little inbreeding to great stud dogs; also keep the pups from chasing rabbits to their holes—it causes the dogs to prop and pull up.

Coursing in public and in private gives to the lover of the sport infinite pleasure, and the study of the breeding and blood of greyhounds is a most fascinating pursuit. All well-bred greyhounds are not good, but all really good greyhounds upon study of their ancestors will be found to be well bred.

XIII

Some Famous Pedigrees

IN choosing the pedigrees for insertion I
have been guided, in my choice of the older
ones, by lines that appear in many of the
present-day pedigrees and which are for the
novice difficult to look up and verify. For the
later years I have taken those of dogs that have
come into "the limelight" of the stud world.
There are probably omissions, not intentional, of
dogs that well deserve a place, but the one idea
in my mind has been to make the series of use
to the novice pedigree lover and they are in no
way intended to be a guide, or list, of the
stud dogs of the present minute.

[PEDIGREES

PEDIGREE I

CANARADZO. Whelped 1858

CANARADZO	Beacon	Blue Light	Monsoon	Colonel Smart
			Stave	Bugle Strawberry
		Frolic	Waterloo	Dusty Miller Exotic
			Clarinda	Cessnock Homet Young
	Scotland Yet	Wigan	Drift	Driver Coquette
			Cutty Sark	Kirkland Cutty Sark
		Veto	Dux	Driver Duppy
			Tillside Lass	Draffin Tillside Lass

Won Waterloo Cup, 1861

PEDIGREE II

MISTERTON. Black. Whelped 1877

MISTERTON					
Contango	Cashier	Cardinal York	Jacobite	Bedlamite	Flounce
			Forest Queen	Ruthless King	Fornarina
		Lady Stormont	Blue Ruin	Antipas	Carolina
			Holiday	Skyrocket	Jailbird
	Bab-at-the-Bowster	Boanerges	Canaradzo	Beacon	Scotland Yet
			Baffle	Hughie Graham	Wild Duck
		Mischief late Bessie Bedlam	Priam	Priam	Virago
			dam	Mynheer	Sis. to Lass o' Gowrie
Lina	Cock Robin	King Death	Canaradzo	Beacon	Scotland Yet
			Annoyance	Heart of Oak	Miss Johnson
		Chloe	Judge	John Bull	Fudge
			Clara	Lopez	Mrs Kitty Brown
	Corinna	Freshman	Combat	Stanley	Moneytaker
			Lively	Forerunner	Linda
		Consequence	David	Motley	Wanton
			Remedy	Mechanic	Ratcatcher's Daughter

Won Waterloo Cup, 1879.

GREENTICK

Black dog. Running weight 64 lbs. Whelped 6th March 1882

GREENTICK	Gen 1	Gen 2	Gen 3	Gen 4	Gen 5	Gen 6
GREENTICK	Bedfellow	Contango	Cashier	Cardinal York	Jacobite	Bedlamite / Florence
					Forest Queen	Ruthless Ki / Fornarino
				Lady Stormont	Blue Ruin	Antipas / Carolina
					Holiday	Skyrocket / Jail Bird
			Bab-at-the-Bowster	Boanerges	Canaradzo	Beacon / Scotland Ye
					Baffle	Hughie Gra / Wild Duck
				Mischief	Priam	Priam / Virago
					Mischief	Mynheer / Sis. to Lass Gowrie
		Bed of Stone	Portland	Effort	Larriston	Liddesdale / Hannah
					Hopmarket	Bedlamite / Cerito
				Prairie Flower	Black Cloud	Blue Light / Frolic
					Prize Flower	Paramount / Isis
			Imperatrice	David	Motley	Sam / Tollwife
					Wanton	Senate / Koket
				Java	Judge	John Bull / Fudge
					Moll Troll	Young Champion / Maid of the Mill
	Heartburn	Blackburn	Lancaster	Cardinal York	Jacobite	Bedlamite / Florence
					Forest Queen	Ruthless Ki / Fornarino
				Hurrara	Sackcloth	Senate / Cinderella
					Winifred	Albert / Barmaid
			Kitty Malone	Canaradzo	Beacon	Blue Light / Frolic
					Scotland Yet	Wigan / Veto
				Kitty Nicholson	Judge	John Bull / Fudge
					Star of the North	Weapon / Unknown
		Nancy	Repealed Hop Duty	Buckshorn	Bedlamite .	Figaro / Bessie Bedl
					Bessie Gregson	.. / ..
				Racketty Hoppicker	Larriston	Liddesdale / Hannah
					Hopbine	Miles / Bloom
			Merry Wife Sis. to Weasel	Patent	David	Motley / Wanton
					Lady Clara	Mansoor / Bess

Won Newton Cup, for puppies, value £330. Ran up for Waterloo Cup, 1884 ; divided Altcar Club Cup into last four for Gosforth Gold Cup, 1885 ; won Palatine Cup at Haydock ; ran up for Gosforth Gold Cup, 188[6]

PEDIGREE IV

HERSCHEL

Red dog. Running weight about 60 lbs. Whelped April 1885

HERSCHEL						
	Mac-Pherson	Master Sam	Contango	Cashier	Cardinal York	Jacobite / Forest Queen
					Lady Stormont	Blue Ruin / Holiday
				Bab-at-the-Bowster	Boanerges	Canaradzo / Baffle
					Mischief	Priam / by Mynheer
			Carlton	Samuel	David	Motley / Wanton
					Patch	Pilgrim / Pandora
				Lucy	Pugilist	Weapon / Pearl
					Cinderella	.. / ..
		Annie Mac-Pherson	Fusilier	Picton	Jacobite	Bedlamite / Flounce
					Forest Queen	Ruthless King / Fornarina
				Blooming Daisy	Judge	John Bull / Fudge
					Fanny Fern	Wigan / The Belle
			Maid of Powhillon	Black Tom	Wellington	Larriston / Consideration
					Bessie ?	Hughie Graham / Rattlesnake
				Miller's Maid	Merry Miller	Sacerdos / ..
					Alice	John Bull / Aunt Annie
	Stargazing II	Canute	Brigade Major	Bendimere	Cauld Kail	Union Jack / Scotia's Thistle
					Bergamot	Sackcloth / Darkness
				Brigade	Brigadier	Boreas / Wee Nell
					Java	Judge / Moll Troll
			Daffodil	Cork Leg	Cauld Kail	Union Jack / Scotia's Thistle
					Tormentor	Coorooan / Honest Lass
				Sis. to S.W.	Crocco	Portsea / Lady Martha
					Indiana	Sea Foam or Derry / Java
		Stargazing	Star and Garter	Rocket	Silkcord	Skyrocket / Silkworm
					Judy	Judge / ..
				Star	Pedigree unknown	.. / ..
			Mrs Cockey	Volunteer	Easy	Let-him-be-Easy / Bessie Graham
					Jessie	.. / ..
				Mischief	Florin	.. / ..
					Skip	.. / ..

vided Haydock Champion Produce Stakes, 137 dogs, winner £500, season 1886-1887 ; won Sefton Stakes at
, 111 entries ; divided Waterloo Cup with his kennel companion, Greater Scot ; and divided Members' Cup
:ar, all in one season. Won Haydock Grand Prize, season 1887-1888 ; won three courses in Waterloo Cup,
ɜ Miss Glendyne in his first course, beaten by Burnaby, the winner, after an undecided ; and the following
 ran into last four for Waterloo Cup, beaten by Fullerton, after being hard run.

207

PEDIGREE V

GALLANT

GALLANT	Young Fullerton	Greentick	(See Pedigree III)	
		Bit of Fashion	Paris	Ptarmigan Gallant Foe
			Pretty Nell	Countryman Sister to Saxon
	Sally Milburn	Misterton	Contango	Cashier Bab-at-the-Bowster
			Lina	Cock Robin Corinna
		Glengowan	Lord of Avon	Pride of Avon Marvel
			Mary Hill	Master Birnie Wee Avon

PEDIGREE VI

PATELEY BRIDGE

PATELEY BRIDGE	Mellor Moor	Monkside	Jester	Ptarmigan Gallant Foe
			Toledo	Reality Terrific
		Miss Birkett	Miner	Æolus Lady Margaret
			Reaction	Bedfellow Lady Glendyne
	Thoughtless Beauty	Herschel	(See Pedigree IV)	
		Thetis	Greentick	(See Pedigree III)
			Tonic	Herrera Terrific

PEDIGREE VII

HOMFRAY. Red. Whelped 1902

HOMFRAY	Fabulous Fortune	Herschel	(See Pedigree IV)	
		Fair Future	Wandering Tom	Willimont-swyke	Banker / Meg o' the Park
				Martha	Benefactor / Venus Aphrodite
			Reformation	Duke of Portland	Caledonia Sunflower
				Reaction	Bedfellow / Lady Glendyne
	Killmode	Restorer	Greentick	(See Pedigree III)	
			Tonic	Herrera	Fugitive Honeydew
				Terrific	Dr Livingstone Flora
		Miss Jessie II	Roderic Dhu	Hubert	Donald Hornet
				Willie's Pet	Tanglethread Speculation Bitch
			Fancy Jane	Dappley Moor	Speculation Forest Flower
				Bugles Eye	Belfast Wicked Eye

Winner of the Waterloo Cup, 1904, as a puppy.

Some Famous Pedigrees

PEDIGREE VIII

DIVIDEND DEFERRED. White and black. Whelped 1903

DIVIDEND DEFERRED	Grampus	Gallant	(See Pedigree V)		
		Gladiole	Mullingar	Misterton	Contango Lina
				Gulnare II	Harfager Herrenhausen
			Sea Serpent	Glenlivet	Highlander Reckless Kate
				Mermaiden	Oversman Siren
	Dark Dame	Fabulous Fortune	Herschel	(See Pedigree IV)	
			Fair Future	Wandering Tom	Willimont-swyke Martha
				Reformation	Duke of Portland Reaction
		Beauteous Bride	Rival Chief	Millington	Misterton Annie MacPherson
				Lady Lizzie	Sir Charles Lizzie
			Moat Terrace	Pandemonium	Phœbus Persephone
				Bird of Beauty	Heir-at-Law Despise

Divided Waterloo Plate in 1905, ran up for Waterloo Cup in 1906, and in following year won three courses in Cup.

PEDIGREE IX
FABER FORTUNÆ

	Herschel	(See Pedigree IV)		
Faber Fortunæ		Wandering Tom	Willimont-swyke	Banker
				Meg o' the Park
			Martha	Benefactor
	Fair Future			Venus Aphrodite
		Reformation	Duke of Portland	Caledonia
				Sunflower
			Reaction	Bedfellow
				Lady Glendyne

PEDIGREE X
MANDINI. Black. Whelped 1903

	Gallant	(See Pedigree V)			
Mandini		Under the Globe	Mullingar	Misterton	Contango
					Lina
				Gulnare II	Harfager
					Herrenhausen
			Sea Serpent	Glenlivet	Highlander
					Reckless Kate
				Mermaiden	Oversman
					Syren
	Kaffir Queen	Fairy Knowe	Monkside	Jester	Ptarmigan
					Gallant Foe
				Toledo	Reality
					Terrific
			Fallacy	Greentick	Bedfellow
					Heartburn
				Foam Bell	Mentor
					Forest Queen

In his three appearances in the Waterloo Cup he was twice in the semi-final and once divided the Plate. Also won Altcar Cup, 1905, and was runner-up for Altcar Club Cup, 1907.

PEDIGREE XI

EARL'S COURT. Red. 70 lb. Whelped 1903

EARL'S COURT	Farndon Ferry	Fiery Furnace	Sir Sankey	Greentick Toledo
			Flying Fancy	Britain Still Fleet Flight
		Fair Florence	Herschel	(See Pedigree IV)
			Fair Future	Wandering Tom Reformation
	Countess Fair	Under the Globe	Mullingar	Misterton Gulnare II
			Sea Serpent	Glenlivet Mermaiden
		Fairy Knowe	Monkside	Jester Toledo
			Fallacy	Greentick Foam Bell

Winner of Benacre Gold Cup (64).

PEDIGREE XII

LOTTERY. Red. 59 lb. Whelped 1904

LOTTERY	Fiery Furnace	Sir Sankey	Greentick	Bedfellow Heartburn
			Toledo	Reality Terrific
		Flying Fancy	Britain Still	Misterton Arama
			Fleet Flight	Fleetfoot Snowffight
	Luck's Reward	Fabulous Fortune	Herschel	MacPherson Stargazing II
			Fair Future	Wandering Tom Reformation
		Beauteous Bride	Rival Chief	Millington Lady Lizzie
			Moat Terrace	Pandemonium Bird of Beauty

As a June puppy Lottery divided the Border Union Derby; he also divided the Waterloo Purse; ran into the semi-finals for Netherby Cup; ran into semi-finals for Waterloo Plate; carried off the Corrie Cup in great style, leading and beating Free Forager pointless in final; ran up for Eye Gold Cup, etc.

PEDIGREE XIII

CHEERS. Fawn. Whelped 1900

CHEERS	Fabulous Fortune	Herschel	Mac-Pherson	Master Sam Annie MacPherson
			Stargazing II	Canute Stargazing
		Fair Future	Wandering Tom	Willimont-swyke Martha
			Reforma-tion	Duke of Portland Reaction
	Real Point	Restorer	Greentick	Bedfellow Heartburn
			Tonic	Herrera Terrific
		Real Lace	Royal King	Clyto Brighton Lady
			Stylish Lady	Misterton Lady Lizzie

PEDIGREE XIV

HOPREND. Fawn. Whelped 1903

HOPREND	Forgotten Fashion	King's Beadsman	Troughend	Greentick Toledo
			Miss Glendyne	Paris Lady Glendyne
		Fairy Fay	Herschel	MacPherson Stargazing II
			Charming Bess	Villiers Cash in Hand
	Heirloom	Under the Globe	Mullingar	Misterton Gulnare II
			Sea Serpent	Glenlivet Mermaiden
		Sleeping Beauty	Forum	Herschel Fine Sport
			Myrtle Green	Warpath Mermaiden

Winner of Waterloo Cup, 1906; Members' Cup, Altcar, 1906; also, after being at the stud, and not thoroughly trained, won three courses in Waterloo Cup, 1907, only then put out by the ultimate winner.

Some Famous Pedigrees

PEDIGREE XV

HOWTOWN.   Brindled.   Whelped 1904

HOWTOWN	Father Flint	Fiery Furnace	Sir Sankey	Greentick Toledo
			Flying Fancy	Britain Still Fleet Flight
		Fanny Faithful	Needham	Herschel Miss Glendyne
			Loyal Maid	Royalty II Leaderess II
	Heirloom	Under the Globe	Mullingar	Misterton Gulnare II
			Sea Serpent	Glenlivet Mermaiden
		Sleeping Beauty	Forum	Herschel Fine Sport
			Myrtle Green	Warpath Mermaiden

The best puppy of his year.   The first five times out divided Ridgway Produce Stakes, Altcar Produce Stakes, Waterloo Plate, and won Clifton Cup (16).

PEDIGREE XVI

DENDRASPIS. Red. 60 lb. Whelped 1905

			Monkside	Jester Toledo
		Mellor Moor		
			Miss Birkett	Miner Reaction
	Wartnaby			
			Herschel	(See Pedigree IV)
		Tiny Polly		
			Thetis	Greentick Tonic
DENDRASPIS				
			Young Fullerton	Greentick Bit of Fashion
		Gallant		
			Sally Milburn	Misterton Glengowan
	Gleneva			
			Mullingar	Misterton Gulnare II
		Gladiole		
			Sea Serpent	Glenlivet Mermaiden

In his first season, won Hornby Castle Cup (32, all ages); second season, divided Altcar Club Cup, won three courses Waterloo Cup, beaten by the winner in fourth round; third season, divided Clifton Cup, won Netherby Cup, won Waterloo Cup.

PEDIGREE XVII

CELERIO. Red. Whelped 1906

				Herschel	MacPherson Stargazing II
CELERIO	Cheers	Fabulous Fortune		Herschel	MacPherson Stargazing II
				Fair Future	Wandering Tom Reformation
		Real Point		Restorer	Greentick Tonic
				Real Lace	Royal King Stylish Lady
	Agile Spurt	Gallant		Young Fullerton	Greentick Bit of Fashion
				Sally Milburn	Misterton Glengowan
		Glen Isla		Plymouth Rock	Carratze Process
				Sea Serpent	Glenlivet Mermaiden

PEDIGREE XVIII

HILLCOURT.   White and brindled.   Whelped 1908

HILLCOURT	Mandini	Gallant	Young Fullerton	Greentick Bit of Fashion
			Sally Milburn	Misterton Glengowan
		Kaffir Queen	Under the Globe	Mullingar Sea Serpent
			Fairy Knowe	Monkside Fallacy
	Camorra	Farndon Ferry	Fiery Furnace	Sir Sankey Flying Fancy
			Fair Florence	Herschel Fair Future
		Thessaly	Falconer	Herschel Fine Sport
			Thetis	Greentick Tonic

PEDIGREE XIX

VICTORIOUS ALLY

Red and fawn. Weight 73 lb. Whelped June 1914

Victorious Ally				
	Silk and Scarlet	Earl's Court	Farndon Ferry	Fiery Furnace Fair Florence
			Countess Fair	Under the Globe Fairy Knowe
		Gay Feather	Real Turk	Falconer Real Lace
			Brown Feather	Featherwood Cairo Belle
	Beacon's Flash	Sky High III	Under the Globe	Mullingar Sea Serpent
			White Lee	Button Park Forest Beauty
		Walton Bonfire	Father o' Fire	Fabulous Fortune Fille de Feu
			Filagree	Stylish Monarch Flutter of Lace

PEDIGREE XX

HOPSACK. Fawn. Whelped 1912

HOPSACK	Hoprend	Forgotten Fashion	King's Beadsman	Troughend	Greentick Toledo
				Miss Glendyne	Paris [dyne Lady Glen-
			Fairy Fay	Herschel	MacPherson Stargazing II
				Charming Bess	Villiers Cash in Hand
		Heirloom	Under the Globe	Mullingar	Misterton Gulnare II
				Sea Serpent	Glenlivet Mermaiden
			Sleeping Beauty	Forum	Herschel Fine Sport
				Myrtle Green	Warpath Mermaiden
	Heart of Freedom	Fight for Freedom	Father Flint	Fiery Furnace	Sir Sankey Flying Fancy
				Fanny Faithful	Needham Loyal Maid
			Fearless Footsteps	Fabulous Fortune	Herschel Fair Future
				Fille de Feu	Greentick Leaderess II
		Quiver II	Spytfontein	Under the Globe	Mullingar Sea Serpent
				Selected	Young Fullerton Rehearsal
			Belle	Seventy-six	Restorer Sprig of Rigmere
				Miss Lowrie	Herschel Glenmahra

Ran up Waterloo Cup 1916.

PEDIGREE XXI

FREE FOOD. Fawn. Whelped 1913

Free Food			
	Friendly Foe	Farndon Ferry	Fiery Furnace Fair Florence
		Satiny	Faber Fortunæ Satin
	Pensa	Gallant	Young Fullerton Sally Milburn
		Pensive Beauty	Mellor Moor Thoughtless Beauty

The Greyhound & Coursing

PEDIGREE XXII

LEGAL LETTER. Fawn. Whelped 1912

LEGAL LETTER				
Postage Paid	Hoprend	Forgotten Fashion	King's Beadsman	Troughend / Miss Glendyne
			Fairy Fay	Herschel / Charming Bess
		Heirloom	Under the Globe	Mullingar / Sea Serpent
			Sleeping Beauty	Forum / Myrtle Green
	Pretty Creature	Boswell	Epicharmus	Jester / Brampton
			Elaine	Restaurant / Eva Jeannie
		Thought-less Beauty	Herschel	MacPherson / Stargazing II
			Thetis	Greentick / Tonic
Love's Reward	Loving Cup	Wang	Skinkle	Seattle / Spence
			Prejudice	Paddington / Process
		Lemon Squash	Coca Wine	Herschel / Coca Water
			Fine Finish	Scoop the Pool / Fair Future
	Luck's Reward	Fabulous Fortune	Herschel	MacPherson / Stargazing II
			Fair Future	Wandering Tom / Reformation
		Beauteous Bride	Rival Chief	Millington / Lady Lizzie
			Moat Terrace	Pandemonium / Bird of Beauty

Some Famous Pedigrees

PEDIGREE XXIII

LUSORY. Red dog. Whelped 1913

LUSORY					
	Friendly Foe	Farndon Ferry	Fiery Furnace	Sir Sankey	Greentick Toledo
				Flying Fancy	Britain Still Fleet Flight
			Fair Florence	Herschel	(See Pedigree IV)
				Fair Future	Wandering Tom Reformation
		Satiny	Faber Fortunæ	(See Pedigree IX)	
			Satin	Under the Globe	Mullingar Sea Serpent
				Selected	Young Fullerton Rehearsal
	Fortuna II	Cheers	Fabulous Fortune	Herschel	(See Pedigree IV)
				Fair Future	Wandering Tom Reformation
			Real Point	Restorer	Greentick Tonic
				Real Lace	Royal King Stylish Lady
		Formula	Pateley Bridge	Mellor Moor	Monkside Miss Birkett
				Thoughtless Beauty	Herschel Thetis
			Forest Fairy	Under the Globe	Mullingar Sea Serpent
				Fantine	Greyfell Miss O'Shea

PEDIGREE XXIV

HARMONICON. Brindled dog. Whelped 1913

HARMONICON	Heavy Weapon	Wartnaby	Mellor Moor	Monkside Miss Birkett
			Tiny Polly	Herschel Thetis
		Garbitas	Gallant	(See Pedigree V)
			Gladiole	Mullingar Sea Serpent
	Camorra	(See under Pedigree XVIII)		

Harmonicon won Waterloo Cup, 1916.

PEDIGREE XXV

HUSKY WHISPER II. Brindled dog. Whelped 1912

HUSKY WHISPER II	Heavy Weapon	(See under Pedigree XXIV)		
	Higher Walton	Benedict	Father Flint	Fiery Furnace Fanny Faithful
			My Lady	King Crispin M. L.
		Formula	(See under Pedigree XXIII)	

226

PEDIGREE XXVI

JULES MUMM. Fawn dog. Whelped 1913

Jules Mumm	Beaded Brow	Earl's Court	(See Pedigree XI)	
		Asphyxy	All About It	Greentick All Alone
			Artery	Fortuna Favente Astery
	Tipula	Father Flint	Fiery Furnace	Sir Sankey Flying Fancy
			Fanny Faithful	Needham Loyal Maid
		Glen Garpool	Gallant	(See Pedigree V)
			Gladiole	Mullingar Sea Serpent

XIV

Coursing Clubs

ENGLAND

N<small>ATIONAL</small> C<small>OURSING</small> C<small>LUB</small>, 11 H<small>AYMARKET</small>, L<small>ONDON</small>, S.W.

A<small>LTCAR</small> C<small>LUB</small>.—Established in 1825 by Lord Molyneux. Originally consisted of twenty ordinary members and four honorary members.

Membership by election, which forms hall-mark of coursing standing.

Meetings held in November and January over Lord Sefton's estates.

Principal Stakes.—Sefton Stakes for dog puppies; Croxteth Stakes for bitch puppies; Altcar Club Cup for all ages; United Produce Stakes; Home-Bred Produce Stakes; Members' Plate.

Best Centres for Meetings.—Liverpool and Southport.

Headquarters.—Exchange Hotel, Liverpool.

Secretary. — John Mugliston, Lytham, Lancs.

BETTISFIELD PARK (Flintshire)—

Local Meeting.

Best Centres.—Oswestry or Ellesmere.

Secretary.—T. Copnall, Hanmer, Whitchurch, Salop.

BODRHYDDAN—

Local Meeting.

Best Centre.—Rhyl.

Headquarters.—Imperial Hotel, Rhyl.

Secretary. — Arthur E. Roberts, Brynterion, Rhyl.

BORDER FARMERS—

Meetings held in October and December.

Principal Stakes. — Netherby Cup for 32 all ages ; Burnfoot Stakes for 16 dog puppies ; Fauld Stakes for 16 bitch puppies.

Best Centre for Meeting.—Carlisle.

Secretary.—Jack Little, Greymoor Hill, Kingstown, Carlisle.

BORDER UNION MEETING—

Meeting held in October over Lord Lonsdale's Lowther estates.

Principal Stakes.—Lonsdale Cup for 32 all ages ; Lowther Stakes for 16 dog puppies ; Whinfell Stakes for 16 bitch puppies.

Best Centre for Meeting.—Penrith.

Headquarters.—George Hotel, Penrith.

Secretary.—Louis Hall, Linden House, Baldwinholme, Carlisle.

BORDER CLUB—

Meetings held at Wooler, Redden, Fenton and other centres in Northumberland.

Principal Stakes.—Wooler Stakes for 16 all ages ; Doddington Stakes for 16 bitch puppies ; Turvelaw Stakes for 16 dog puppies.

Best Centres for Meetings.—Alnwick or Kelso.

Secretary.—J. Gibson, Bentinck House, Ashington, Northumberland.

BOTHAL CLUB—

One of the oldest Coursing Clubs in existence.

Meetings held occasionally.

Best Centre.—Newcastle.

Secretary.—Captain Ellis, Bothalhaugh, Morpeth.

Coursing Clubs

BRIGG.—(See ELSHAM and WORLABY).

BRYN-Y-PYS—

Local Meeting, held over Major Hugh E. Peel's and Lord Kenyon's estates.

Best Centre.—Wrexham.

Secretary. — W. B. Mitchell, Overton, Ellesmere, Salop.

CRAMLINGTON (Northumberland)—

Local Meeting, held over estates of Lord Cramlington.

Best Centre.—Newcastle.

Secretary.—R. Reilly, Blagdon Terrace, Cramlington.

DARLINGTON AND BISHOP AUCKLAND—

Local Meeting.

Best Centre.—Darlington.

Secretary.—A. Graham, 8 Victoria Embankment, Darlington.

DINWOODIE (Lockerbie)—

Local Meeting, run over Sir R. B. Jardine's estates.

Best Centre.—Lockerbie.

Secretary.—D. W. Campbell, Breckonhill, Lockerbie, N.B.

ELSHAM AND WARLABY (Brigg)—

Local Meeting.

Best Centre.—Brigg.

Secretary.—J. Ashton, Woolpack Hotel, Brigg.

GREDINGTON—

Local Meeting.

Best Centre.—Overton.

Secretary. — W. B. Mitchell, Overton, Ellesmere, Salop.

HADDON AND CHATSWORTH—

Run over the estates of Lord Hartington and the Marquis of Granby.

Principal Stakes. — Peveril Cup for all ages ; Granby Cup for puppies.

Best Centre.—Matlock.

Secretary.—Mr Clark.

HARTFORD, NEDDERTON AND DISTRICT (Northumberland)—

Local Meetings.

Best Centre.—

Secretary.—

Coursing Clubs

HEREFORDSHIRE CLUB—
    Local Meetings.
    Best Centres.—Ross and Hereford.
    Headquarters.—Black Swan, Hereford.
    Secretary.—W. H. Brian, Black Swan, Hereford.

HETT HILLS (Durham)—
    Local Meeting.
    Best Centre.—Durham.
    Secretary.—F. Walker, Brunswick Hotel, Stockton-on-Tees.

HOCKWOLD AND FELTWELL (Norfolk)—
    Almost an enclosed Meeting.
    Principal Stakes.—Norfolk County Cup for all ages ; Field Farm Stakes for puppies.
    Best Centres.—Norwich and Thetford.
    Secretary.— A. E. Watson, Myntlyn House, Hockwold, Norfolk.

NEWMARKET.—(See SOUTHERN COUNTIES).

NORFOLK AND NORWICH—
    Local.
    Best Centre.—Norwich.
    Secretary.—W. Daplyn, Elm Farm, Little Melton, Norwich.

OVINGTON (Northumberland)—

Local Meetings.

Best Centre.—

Secretary. — G. Robertson, Ovington, Northumberland.

PENSHAW AND GRINDON—

Local.

Best Centre.—Durham.

Secretary.—J. Handy, Nag's Head, Houghton-le-Spring.

RABY TENANTS'—

Local, run over Lord Barnard's estates.

Best Centre.—Piercebridge.

Secretary.—J. Porter, High Moor House, Ingleton, Darlington.

ROKEBY—

Local.

Best Centre.—Barnard Castle.

Secretary.—C. Hedley Hunter, 17 Galgate, Barnard Castle.

SOUTHERN COUNTIES—

Meetings at Cheddington, over Lord Rosebery's estates ; Chelmsford, Newmarket, etc.

Principal Stakes. — Cheddington Cup ; Derby Stakes ; Oaks Stakes ; Model Farm Stakes.

Best Centre.—Leighton Buzzard.

Secretary.—T. B. Rixon, 11 Copthal Court, London, E.C.

SOUTH LANCASHIRE—

Meetings twice in season over Scarisbrick estates.

Principal Stakes.—Scarisbrick Cup for all ages ; North Meols Cup for puppies ; Southport Stakes ; Manor Stakes.

Best Centres.—Liverpool or Southport.

Headquarters.—Railway Hotel, Southport.

Secretary.—W. Graham, Churchtown, Southport.

SUSSEX COUNTY—

Meetings held at Aldingbourne, Bognor and Petworth.

Membership Fee.—Five Guineas.

Principal Stakes.—Sussex County Derby ; Sussex County Oaks ; Produce Sweepstakes ; Fighting Force Cup ; Hobgen Champion Stakes, etc.

At present this Club endows bigger stakes than any other Club in England.

Best Centre.—Bognor.

Headquarters.—Royal Norfolk Hotel, Bognor.

Secretary.—J. H. Skinner, Strood Farm, Petworth.

WEST RAINTON TENANTS'—

Local.

Best Centre.—Durham.

Secretary.—John Bailey, Fence Houses, Durham.

WINDLESTONE—

Local.

Best Centre.—Durham.

Secretary.—D. S. Pearce, The Rookery, Ferryhill, Durham.

WRYDE CLUB—

Run over Fen district near Peterborough.

Membership Fee.—Two Guineas.

Principal Stakes.—Barbican Cup ; Wryde Derby ; Thorney Oaks.

Best Centre.—Peterborough.

Headquarters.—Grand Hotel, Peterborough.

Secretary.—H. Hurry, Angel Hotel, Peterborough.

Coursing Clubs

IRELAND

The most important meetings are :

Clonmel and Kilsheelan—

Principal Stakes. — Castle Stakes for puppies ; Ballyglasheen Stakes for all ages ; Kilsheelan Stakes for second seasons ; Anner Stakes for all ages.

Secretary.—A. O'Shea, The Courthouse, Clonmel.

Cork—

Principal Stakes.—Bracelet Stakes for 32 puppies ; Blackrock Stakes for 32 all ages ; Ballintemple Stakes for 32 all ages ; Beaumont Stakes for 32 all ages ; Cork Cup for 64 all ages ; Cork Purse ; Cork Plate.

Secretary.—G. Hutchinson, Lavitt's Quay, Cork.

County Louth and West Meath—

Principal Stakes.—Duggan Cup for 64 all ages ; Purse ; Plate.

Secretary.—P. Halfpenny, Ardee, County Louth.

DROGHEDA AND DISTRICT—

Principal Stakes. — Mornington Stakes; for puppies. Tredagh Stakes for all ages.

Secretary.—Jas. Robinson, Trinity Street, Drogheda.

LIMERICK—

Principal Stakes.—Irish Cup for 64 all ages; Purse; Plate.

Secretary.—E. O. Reardon, Glencore.

MARYBOROUGH—

Principal Stakes.—Midland Cup; Blake Stakes; Shaen Stakes; Castle Stakes.

Secretary.—

NORTHERN COURSING CLUB—

Principal Stakes.—Aldergrove Stakes for bitch puppies; Ballycraigy Stakes for dog puppies; Ballinderry Stakes for all ages; Lough Neagh Stakes for all ages.

Centre.—Massereene Park.

Secretary. — P. Meenan, 4 Prince Chambers, 72 Ann Street, Belfast.

QUEEN'S COUNTY—

Principal Stake.—Queen's County Cup.

Secretary.—G. N. Jessop, Maryborough, Queen's County.

TRALEE—

Principal Stakes.—Kingdom Cup for 64 all ages ; Purse ; Plate.

Secretary.—J. B. Rice, 14 Bridge Street, Tralee.

XV

Rules of the National Coursing Club

1. THE SECRETARY AND STEWARDS.—For any proposed Open Meeting a Committee of not less than three shall be formed, who, with the Secretary, shall settle preliminaries. The management of the Meeting shall be entrusted to this Committee, in conjunction with Stewards who shall be elected by the subscribers present at the first evening of meeting. The Secretary, if honorary, shall be a member of the Committee and a Steward *ex officio*. The Stewards alone shall decide any disputed question by a majority of those present, subject to an appeal to the National Coursing Club. No Steward shall have a right to vote in any case relating to his own dogs. The Secretary shall declare, on or before the evening preceding the last day's running, how the prizes are to be divided; and shall give a statement of expenses, if called upon to do so by any six of the subscribers, within fourteen days after the meeting. No stakes shall be paid until fourteen days after the completion of a meeting; but all stakes must be paid within thirty days.

2. Ex-officio Stewards.—Members of the National Coursing Club present at any Coursing Meeting shall be *ex-officio* Stewards of such Meeting, together with the Stewards elected by the subscribers present on the first evening of the meeting, provided always that such Stewards *ex officio* shall not exceed three. Members of the National Coursing Club may be elected by the subscribers as Stewards of a meeting.

3. Election of Judge. — The Judge may either be appointed by the Secretary and Committee acting under Rule 1, in which case his name shall be announced simultaneously with the meeting, or elected by the votes of the subscribers taking nominations ; but each subscriber shall have only one vote, whatever the number of his nominations. Not less than ten days' notice of the day of election shall be given to the subscribers, and the appointment shall be published at least a fortnight before the meeting. The names of the subscribers voting, with the votes given by them, shall be recorded in a book open to the inspection of the Stewards, who shall declare the number of votes for each Judge, if called upon to do so by any of the subscribers. When a Judge is prevented from attending or finishing a meeting, the Committee and the Stewards (if appointed) shall have the power of deciding what is to be done.

4. Description of Entry.—Every subscriber

to a stake must name his dog before the time fixed for closing the entry, giving the names (the running names if they had any) of the sire and dam of the dog entered. The Secretary shall publish on the cards the names of those who are subscribers, but do not comply with these conditions. These nominations shall not be drawn, but must be paid for. For Produce Stakes the names, pedigrees, ages, colours, and distinguishing marks of puppies, shall be detailed in writing to the Secretary of a meeting at the time of the original entry in all Puppy Stakes, and a subscriber must, if required, state in writing to the Secretary, before or during the meeting for which such entry is made, the names and addresses of the parties who reared his puppies ; and any puppy whose marks and pedigree shall be proved not to correspond with the entry given shall be disqualified, and the whole of its stakes or winnings forfeited. No greyhound is to be considered a puppy which was whelped before the first of January of the year preceding the commencement of the season of running. A sapling is a greyhound whelped on or after the first of January of the year in which the season of running commenced.

5. REGISTRATION.—Every litter of Puppies shall within two months of the date of whelping be registered at a fee of 1s. 6d., with the names of sire and dam, and the colour (subject to cor-

rection within six months after the date of whelping), sex, and number of the Puppies, under a penalty of £1, with a further fee of 5s. to 30th June for Registration at the time of naming each Puppy not registered under the above requirements. In cases where the last registered owner of the dam and the owner of the whelps is not identical, the written consent of the registered owner of the dam must be obtained. All Greyhounds must be named and registered in the *Stud Book* with the Names of their owners, Colours, Sex, Names and Pedigree, and the Names of owners of their sire and dam. The Registration Fee shall be 1s. 6d. for each dog named and registered on or before 30th June. Any subsequent registration (except saplings) will be subject to a penalty of £1 up to a period of two years of the date of whelping, after which the penalty will be £5. Every change of ownership must be registered at a fee of 5s. within one month under a penalty of £1, before any Greyhound shall be eligible to run or be used for breeding purposes. The production of the previous certificate or written consent of the previous registered owner is compulsory before re-registration except in the case where the dog has been purchased by public auction at the Royal Barbican Repository.

6. STUD BOOK.—The *Greyhound Stud Book* shall be published, under the authority of the

National Coursing Club, on the 15th day of September.

7. TIME FOR REGISTRATION.—The Registration of Greyhounds shall be made on or before the 30th day of June, and Registrations made after that date, if they do not appear in the *Stud Book* of that year, will appear in that of the following year.

8. NAMES.—If the same name has been given to more than one greyhound, the Keeper of the *Stud Book* shall give priority to the dog first registered, and shall add to every other such name, except the one first registered, a numeral, commencing with II. Names once used will not be again available until after a lapse of ten years. Provided that should a greyhound die before it has run, or has been bred from, and notice thereof is within one month given to the Keeper of the *Stud Book*, the name of such greyhound shall be at once available by the same owner for another greyhound.

9. GREYHOUNDS NOT REGISTERED ARE DISQUALIFIED.—All Greyhounds whose names do not appear in the *Stud Book*, or whose owners cannot produce a Certificate of Registration from the Keeper of the *Stud Book* on being required to do so by a Steward, or the Secretary of any Coursing Meeting, shall be disqualified, and shall forfeit all Entry Money which may have been paid, and any Stake or Prize, or Share of any

Stake or Prize won at such Meeting, and such Entry Money, Stake, or Prize, or Share thereof won by any Dog so disqualified, shall be disposed of as provided by Rule 38 applicable to disqualification.

10. PAYMENT OF ENTRY MONEY.—All moneys due for nominations taken must be paid at or before the time fixed for closing the entry, whether the stakes fill or not, and although, from insufficient description or any other cause, the dogs named may be disqualified. No entry shall be valid unless the amount due for it has been paid in full. For all Produce and other Stakes, where a forfeit is payable, no declaration is necessary ; the non-payment of the remainder of the entry money at the time fixed for that purpose is to be considered a declaration of forfeit. The Secretary is to be responsible for the entry money of all dogs whose names appear upon the card.

11. ALTERATION OF NAME.—If any subscriber should enter a Greyhound by a different name from that in which it shall have last been entered to run in public he shall give notice of the alteration to the Secretary at the time of entry, and the Secretary shall place on the card both the late and the present names of the dog, and this must be done at all meetings at which the dog runs throughout the ensuing season. If notice of the alteration be not given, the dog shall be disqualified.

The new name must be registered before the dog can run under it.

12. PREFIX OF " Ns."—Any subscriber taking an entry in a stake must prove to the satisfaction of the Stewards, if called upon by them to do so, that any Greyhound entered by him, without the prefix of the word " Names," is *bona fide* his own property. If a subscriber enters a dog not his own property, without putting " ns " after his own name, the dog so entered shall be disqualified. Every subscriber shall, if requested, deliver in writing to the Secretary of the Meeting the name of the *bona fide* owner of the Greyhound named by him, and this communication is to be produced should any dispute arise. No dog purchased or procured for a less time than the entire period still remaining of its public running, or belonging to two or more persons, unless they are declared confederates, shall be held as *bona fide* the property of a subscriber. A copy of the lease of a greyhound, registered or re-registered, must be lodged with the Keeper of the *Stud Book* at the time of such registration and re-registration. The names of confederates must be registered with the Keeper of the *Stud Book*—fee, one shilling for each name. Assumed names must also be registered with the Keeper of the *Stud Book*—fee, five guineas.

13. DEATH OF A SUBSCRIBER.—The death of a subscriber shall only affect his nominations if

it occurs before the draw, in which case, subject to the exceptions stated below, they shall be void, whether the entries have been made or not, and any money received for forfeits or stakes shall be returned, less the proportion of expenses when the amount has been advertised, and when the nominations rendered vacant are not filled by other subscribers. If he has parted with all interest in the nominations, and dogs not his property are entered and paid for, such entries shall not subsequently be disturbed. When dogs that have been entered in Produce Stakes change owners, with their engagements and with their forfeits paid, the then owner, if entitled to run them in those stakes, shall not be prevented from doing so by reason of the death of the former owner.

14. DRAW. — Immediately before the greyhounds are drawn at any meeting, and before nine o'clock on every subsequent evening during the continuance of such meeting, the time and place of putting the first brace of dogs into the slips on the following morning shall be declared. A card or counter bearing a corresponding number shall be assigned to each entry. These numbered cards or counters shall then be placed together, and drawn indiscriminately. This classification, once made, shall not be disturbed throughout the meeting, except for the purpose of guarding, or on account of byes.

15. GUARDING.—When two or more nominations in a stake are taken in one name, the greyhounds, if *bona fide* the property of the same owner, shall be guarded throughout. This is always to be arranged, if possible, by bringing up dogs from below to meet those which are to be guarded. This guarding is not, however, to deprive any dog of a natural bye to which he may be entitled, either in the draw, or in running through the stake. The withdrawal at any time of a dog from a stake shall not deprive a dog of a bye, accidental or natural, to which it would have been entitled had the withdrawn dog remained in the stake. Dogs, whose position has been altered in consequence of guarding or of byes, must return to their original position in the next round, if guarding does not prevent it.

16. BYES.—A natural bye shall be given to the lowest available dog in each round. No dog shall run a second such bye in any stake, unless it is unavoidable. When a dog is entitled to a bye, either natural or accidental, his owner or nominator may run any greyhound he pleases to assist in the course, provided always that in Sapling Stakes only a sapling may be used, and in Puppy Stakes none older than a puppy. But if it is proved to the satisfaction of the Stewards that no sapling or puppy respectively can be found to run an accidental bye, an older dog may be used. No dog shall run any bye earlier

than his position entitles him to do. The slip and the course in a bye shall be the same as in a course in which a decision is required, and the Judge shall decide whether enough has been done to constitute a course, or whether it must be run again, and in the latter case the Judge shall give the order. If at the commencement of any round in a stake, one dog in each course of that round has a bye, those byes shall not be run, but the dogs shall take their places for the next round as if the byes had been run. A bye must be run before a dog can claim the advantage of it. Byes or participation in winnings, through being entitled to byes, shall count as courses won.

17. SLIP STEWARD.—The Committee of an open meeting and the members of a club meeting shall appoint, on the first evening of a meeting, a Slip Steward, whose duty shall be to see that the right greyhounds, both in courses and byes, are brought to slips in their proper turn ; to report to the Stewards, without delay, any greyhound that does not come to the slips in time, and any act on the part of the slipper, nominators, or their representatives, which he may consider should be brought to their knowledge. If a nominator or his representative should refuse to comply with the directions of Slip Steward, or should use abusive or insulting or threatening language towards him, he shall be at once

reported to the Standing Committee. A Slip Steward cannot be both Slip Steward and Flag Steward at any coursing meeting.

18. POSTPONEMENT OF MEETING.—A meeting appointed to take place on a certain day may, if a majority of the Committee and the Stewards (if appointed) consider the weather unfit for coursing, be postponed from day to day; but if the running does not commence within the current week all nominations shall be void, unless it shall be especially stated otherwise in the conditions of the meeting or in the conditions of a Special Stake or Prize at such meeting, and the expenses shall be paid by the subscribers, in proportion to the value of nominations taken by each. In the case of Produce Stakes, however, the original entries shall continue binding if the meeting is held at a later period of the season.

19. TAKING DOGS TO THE SLIPS.—Every dog must be brought to the slips in its proper turn, without delay, under a penalty of £1. If absent for more than ten minutes (according to the report of the Slip Steward or of one of the Stewards), its opponent shall be entitled to claim the course, subject to the discretion of the Stewards, and shall in that case run a bye. If both dogs be absent at the expiration of ten minutes, the Stewards shall have power to disqualify both dogs, or to fine their owners any sum not exceeding £5 each. The nominator is

answerable for his dog being put into the slips at the right time, and on the right side. No allowance shall be made for mistakes ; but it the wrong dogs shall have run together in any round, and the mistake has not been discovered until another round has been run, no objection can be made, and the courses must stand as run. No dog shall be put into the slips for a deciding course until thirty minutes after its course in the previous round without the consent of its owner (see Rule 32).

20. CONTROL OF DOGS IN SLIPS.—The control of all matters connected with slipping the greyhounds, or permitting them to be placed in slips, shall rest with the Stewards of a meeting. Owners or servants, after delivering their dogs into the hands of the Slipper, may follow close after them, but not so as to inconvenience the Slipper, or in any way interfere with the dogs. Neither must they holloa them on while running. An owner, trainer, or attendant, after putting his dog in slips, may go forward to catch his dog, but must keep well clear of the line on the run of the hare, and must go forward on the same side as his dog is in the slips, except in such cases that the Stewards shall decide that it is advisable for both parties to go forward on the same side. Anyone infringing this rule may be fined a sum not exceeding £5, at the discretion of the Stewards. Any greyhound found

to be beyond control in slips may, by order of the Stewards, be taken out of the slips and disqualified.

21. GREYHOUNDS OF SAME COLOUR TO WEAR COLLARS.—When two greyhounds drawn together are of the same colour, they shall each wear a collar, and the owners shall be subject to a penalty of ten shillings for non-observance of this rule. The colour of the collar shall be red for the left-hand side and white for the right-hand side of the slips. The upper dog on the card must be placed on the left hand, and the lower dog on the right hand of the slips.

22. THE SLIP.—The order to slip may be given by the Judge, or the Slip Steward, or the Stewards of a meeting may leave the slip to the sole discretion of the Slipper. The length of slip must necessarily vary with the nature of the ground, but should never be less than from three to four score yards, and must be maintained of one uniform length, as far as possible, throughout each stake.

23. THE SLIPPER.—If one greyhound gets out of the slips the Slipper shall not let the other go. In any case of slips breaking, and either or both dogs getting away in consequence, the Slipper may be fined a sum not exceeding £1, at the discretion of the Stewards.

24. DECISION OF THE JUDGE.—The Judge shall be subject to the General Rules which may be

Rules

established by the National Coursing Club for his guidance. He shall, on the termination of each course, immediately deliver his decision aloud, and shall not recall or reverse his decision, on any pretext whatever, after it has been declared ; but no decision shall be delivered until the Judge is perfectly satisfied that the course is absolutely terminated.

25. PRINCIPLES OF JUDGING.—The Judge shall decide all courses upon the one uniform principle that the greyhound which does most towards killing the hare during the continuance of the course is to be declared the winner. The principle is to be carried out by estimating the value of the work done by each greyhound, as seen by the Judge, upon a balance of points according to the scale hereafter laid down, from which also are to be deducted certain specified allowances and penalties.

26. The points of the course are—

  a. *Speed*—which shall be estimated as one, two, or three points, according to the degree of superiority shown (see definition below, *a*).

  b. *The Go-bye.*—Two points, or if gained on the outer circle, three points.

  c. *The Turn.*—One point.

  d. *The Wrench.*—Half-a-point.

  e. *The Kill.*—Two points, or, in a descending scale, in proportion to the degree of merit displayed in that kill, which may be of no value.

  f. *The Trip.*—One point.

253

The Greyhound & Coursing

a. In estimating the value of speed to the hare the Judge must take into account the several forms in which it may be displayed—viz.

1. Where in the run up a clear lead is gained by one of the dogs, in which case one, two, or three points may be given, according to the length of lead, apart from the score for a turn or wrench. In awarding these points the Judge shall take into consideration the merit of a lead obtained by a dog which has lost ground at the start, either from being unsighted, or from a bad slip, or which has had to run the outer circle.

2. Where one greyhound leads the other so long as the hare runs straight, but loses the lead from her bending round decidedly in favour of the slower dog of her own accord, in which case the one greyhound shall score one point for the speed shown, and the other dog score one point for the first turn.

3. Under no circumstances is speed without subsequent work to be allowed to decide a course, except where great superiority is shown by one greyhound over another in a long lead to covert.

If a dog, after gaining the first six points, still keeps possession of the hare by superior speed, he shall have double the prescribed allowance for the subsequent points made before his opponent begins to score.

b. The Go-bye is where a greyhound starts a clear length behind his opponent and yet passes him in a straight run, and gets a clear length before him.

c. The Turn is where the hare is brought round at not less than a right angle from her previous line.

254

d. The Wrench is where the hare is bent from her line at less than a right angle; but where she only leaves her line to suit herself, and not from the greyhound pressing her, nothing is to be allowed.

e. The Merit of a Kill must be estimated according to whether a greyhound, by his own superior dash and skill, bears the hare; whether he picks her up through any little accidental circumstances favouring him, or whether she is turned into his mouth, as it were, by the other greyhound.

f. The Trip, or unsuccessful effort to kill, is where the hare is thrown off her legs, or where a greyhound flecks her, but cannot hold her.

27. The following allowances shall be made for accidents to a greyhound during a course; but in every case they shall only be deducted from the other dog's score :—

a. For losing ground at the start, either from being un-sighted, or from a bad slip, in which case the Judge is to decide what amount of allowance is to be made, on the principle that the score of the foremost dog is not to begin until the second has had an opportunity of joining in the course, and the Judge may decide the course or declare the course to be an undecided or no course, as he may think fit.

b. Where a hare bears very decidedly in favour of one of the greyhounds, after the first or subsequent turns, in which case the next point shall not be scored by the dog unduly favoured, or only half his points allowed, according to circumstances. No greyhound shall receive any allowance for a fall or an accident, with the exception of being ridden over by the owner of the competing greyhound, or his servant, provided for by Rule 31, or when pressing his hare, in which case his opponent shall not count the next point made.

The Greyhound & Coursing

28. PENALTIES—

a. Where a greyhound, from his own defect, refuses to
follow the hare at which he is slipped, he shall lose
the course.

b. Where a dog wilfully stands still in a course, or
departs from directly pursuing the hare, no points
subsequently made by him shall be scored; and if
the points made by him up to that time be just equal
to those made by his antagonist in the whole course,
he shall thereby lose the course; but where one or
both dogs stop with the hare in view, through inability
to continue the course, it shall be decided according
to the number of points gained by each dog during
the whole course.

c. If a dog refuses to fence where the other fences, any
points subsequently made by him are not to be scored;
but if he does his best to fence, and is foiled by sticking in a muse, the course shall end there. When the
points are equal, the superior fencer shall win the
course.

29. SECOND HARE.—If a second hare be
started during a course, and one of the dogs
follows her, the course shall end there.

30. GREYHOUND GETTING LOOSE.—Any person allowing a greyhound to get loose, and join
in a course which is being run, shall be fined
£1. If the loose greyhound belong to either
of the owners of the dogs engaged in the particular course, such owner shall forfeit his chance
of the stake with the dog then running, unless
he can prove, to the satisfaction of the Stewards,
that he had not been able to get the loose greyhound taken up after running its own course.

256

The course is not to be considered as necessarily ended when a third dog joins in.

31. RIDING OVER A GREYHOUND.—If any subscriber, or his servant, shall ride over his opponent's greyhound while running a course, the owner of the dog so ridden over shall (although the course be given against him) be deemed the winner of it, or shall have the option of allowing the other dog to remain and run out the stake, and in such case shall be entitled to half its winnings.

32. NO COURSE.—A "no course" is when by accident or by the shortness of the course the dogs are not tried together, and if one be then drawn the other must run a bye, unless the Judge on being appealed to shall decide that he has done enough work to be exempted from it. An undecided course is where the Judge considers the merits of the dogs equal, and if either is then drawn, the other cannot be required to run a bye; but the owners must at the time declare which dog remains in (see Rule 34). The Judge shall signify the distinction between a "no course" and an "undecided" by taking off his hat in the latter case only. After an undecided or no course, if the dogs before being taken up get on another or the same hare, the Judge must follow, and shall decide in favour of one if he considers that there has been a sufficient trial to justify his doing so.

A " no course " or an " undecided " may be run
off immediately, if claimed on behalf of both
dogs before the next brace are put into the
slips, or in case of " no course," if so ordered
by the Judge, otherwise it shall be run again
after the two next courses, unless it stand over
till the next morning, when it shall be the first
course run ; if it is the last course of the day,
fifteen minutes shall be allowed after both dogs
are taken up.

33. EXPLANATION BY JUDGE. — The Judge
shall render an explanation of any decision only
to the Stewards of the meeting if required,
through them, before the third succeeding
course, by the owner, or nominator, or representative of the owner or nominator, of either
of the greyhounds engaged in the course. The
Stewards shall, if requested to do so, express
their opinion whether the explanation is satisfactory or not, and their opinion in writing
may be asked for and published afterwards, but
the decision of the Judge, once given, shall not
be reversed for any cause.

34. WITHDRAWAL OF A DOG.—If a dog be
withdrawn from any stake on the field, its owner,
or someone having his authority, must at once
give notice to the Secretary or Flag or Slip
Steward. If the dog belongs to either of these
officials, the notice must be given to the other.
When after a no course or an undecided one

of the greyhounds has been officially drawn, and the dogs are again, by mistake, put into the slips and run a course, the arrangements come to shall stand, whatever the Judge's decision may be, and all bets on the course shall be void.

35. IMPUGNING JUDGE.—If any subscriber, owner, or any other person, proved to be interested, openly impugns the decision of the Judge on the ground, except by a complaint to the Stewards, according to Rule 33, he shall forfeit not more than £5, nor less than £2, at the discretion of the Stewards.

36. STAKES NOT RUN OUT.—When two greyhounds remain in for the deciding course, the stakes shall be considered divided if they belong to the same owner, or to confederates, and also if the owner of one of the two dogs induces the owner of the other to draw him for any payment or consideration ; but if one of the two be drawn without payment or consideration, from lameness, or from any cause clearly affecting his chance of winning, the other may be declared the winner, the facts of the case being clearly proved to the satisfaction of the Stewards. The same rule shall apply when more than two dogs remain in at the end of a stake which is not run out ; and in case of a division between three or more dogs, of which two or more belong to the same owner,

these latter shall be held to take equal shares
of the total amount received by their owner in
a division. When there is a compulsory division, all greyhounds remaining in the class
that is being run, even where one is entitled
to a bye, shall take equal shares. The terms
of any arrangement to divide winnings, and the
amount of any money given to induce the owner
of a dog to draw him, must be declared to the
Secretary.

37. WINNERS OF STAKES RUNNING TOGETHER.
—If two or more greyhounds shall each win a
stake, and have to run together for a final prize
or challenge cup, should they not have run an
equal number of ties in their respective stakes,
the greyhound which has run the smaller
number of courses must run a bye, or byes, to
put itself upon an equality in this respect with
its opponent.

38. OBJECTIONS. — An objection to a greyhound may be made to any one of the Stewards
of a meeting at any time before the stakes are
paid over, upon the objector lodging in the
hands of such Steward, or the Secretary, the
sum of £5, which shall be forfeited if the objection proves frivolous, or if he shall not bring
the case before the next meeting of the National
Coursing Club, or give notice to the Stewards
previous thereto of his intention to withdraw
the objection. The owner of the greyhound

objected to must deposit equally the sum of £5, and prove the correctness of his entry. Expenses in consequence of an objection shall be borne as the National Coursing Club may direct. Should an objection be made which cannot at the time be substantiated or disproved, the greyhound may be allowed to run under protest, the Stewards retaining the winnings until the objection has been withdrawn, or heard and decided. If the greyhound objected to be disqualified, the amount to which he would otherwise have been entitled shall be divided equally among the dogs beaten by him ; and if a piece of plate or prize has been added, and won by him, only the dogs which he beat in the several rounds shall have a right to contend for it.

39. DEFAULTERS.—No person to whom Rule 41, as hereinafter has been applied, or who is a defaulter for either stakes, forfeits, or bets, or for money due under an arrangement for a division of winnings, or for penalties regularly imposed for the infraction of Rules by the Stewards of any meeting, or for any payment required by a decision of the National Coursing Club, or for subscriptions due to any club entitled to have representatives in the National Coursing Club shall be allowed to enter or run a greyhound, in his own or any other person's name, or attend any coursing meeting,

or the draw, dinner, or calling over of the card of any meeting. As regards bets, however, this rule shall only apply when a complaint is lodged with the Secretary of the National Coursing Club within six months after the bet becomes due. On receipt of such complaint the Secretary shall give notice of the claim to the person against whom it is made, with a copy of this rule, and if he should not pay the bet, or appear before the next meeting of the National Coursing Club, and resist the claim successfully, he shall be considered a defaulter.

40. JUDGE OR SLIPPER INTERESTED. — If a Judge or Slipper be in any way interested in the winnings of a greyhound or greyhounds, the owner and nominator in each case, unless they can prove satisfactorily that such interest was without their cognisance, shall forfeit all claim to the winnings, and the dog shall be disqualified ; and if any nominator or owner of greyhounds shall give, offer, or lend money, or anything of value, to any Judge or Slipper, such owner or nominator shall not be allowed to run dogs in his own or any other person's name during any subsequent period that the National Coursing Club may decide upon.

41. DISCREDITABLE CONDUCT. — Any person who is proved to the satisfaction of the National Coursing Club to have been guilty of any fraudulent or discreditable conduct in connection with

coursing, or any other recognised sport, may, in addition to any pecuniary penalty to which he may be liable, be declared incapable of running or entering a greyhound in his own or any other person's name during any subsequent period that the National Coursing Club may decide upon ; and any dogs under his care, training, management, or superintendence shall be disqualified during such subsequent period.

42. BETS.—All bets upon an undecided course shall stand unless one of the greyhounds be drawn. All bets upon a dog running farther than another in the stake shall be p.p., whatever accident may happen. Bets upon a deciding, as upon every other course, are off if the course is not run. Long odd bets shall be void when made after the draw unless the greyhound the bet refers to shall run one course in the Stake, other than a bye, after the bet is made. In the case of a meeting, or of a coursing prize, where the nominations are not void in consequence of postponement, all long odd bets made before the first draw shall hold good, but long odd bets made after any draw, except the draw under which the stake is run, shall be void.

43. BETS ON STAKES DIVIDED. — Where money has been laid against a dog winning a stake, and he divides it, the two sums must be put together and divided in the same proportion as the value of the stakes.

The Greyhound & Coursing

Since this book went to press the following amendments have been made to Rules 21 and 24 by the National Coursing Club :—

1. Dogs will invariably wear collars.
2. Judges will still have the option of calling their decisions aloud if and when they find it easier to distinguish the dogs by their colours rather than by the collars they are wearing.
3. Under no circumstances must the colours of the collars be called aloud.

INDEX

Index

Index

Index

Index

Index

Index

Lightning Source UK Ltd.
Milton Keynes UK
UKOW040607090512

192175UK00001B/50/P